Daily Math
Warm-Ups
Grade Five

by
Marilyn Preddy

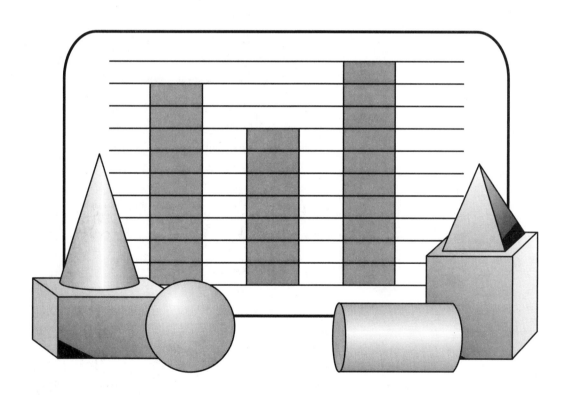

Carson-Dellosa Publishing Company, Inc.
Greensboro, North Carolina

Credits

Editors
Hank Rudisill
Sabena Maiden

Cover Design
Dez Perrotti

Cover Photo
Comstock, Inc.

Layout Design
Hank Rudisill

Art Coordinator
Betsy Peninger

Artists
Jon Nawrocik
Julie Kinlaw

This book has been correlated to state, national, and Canadian provincial standards. Visit *www.carsondellosa.com* to search for and view its correlations to your standards.

ISBN 0-88724-821-7

Table of Contents
Daily Math Warm-Ups Grade Five

Introduction to *Daily Math Warm-Ups*

Based on standards specified by the National Council of Teachers of Mathematics (NCTM), *Daily Math Warm-Ups* will give teachers a year-long collection of challenging problems that reinforce math skills taught in the classroom. Designed around the traditional school year, the series offers 180 daily lessons (sets of five problems each) including computation, graph, and word problems. For each two-week group of lessons, an eight-problem multiple-choice assessment is provided to help you easily identify which students have mastered which concepts. The daily practice will help improve students' skills and bolster their confidence.

How to Use This Book

You can use this book in the following ways:
- Use the problems as a daily math warm-up. Make each child responsible for keeping a math journal that is checked periodically. Copy the daily lessons on transparencies. At the beginning of each class, put the problems on an overhead and give students approximately five minutes to solve the problems. When students have completed the exercise, go over the problems as a class. You can use this opportunity to discuss why some answers are correct and others are not.
- Because copying from the board or overhead is challenging for some learners, you may choose to photocopy the daily lessons for particular students, or for the entire class. Have students work on the problems at the beginning of class, then continue as described above.
- Give each student a copy of the problems near the end of class and have them turn the work in as a "Ticket Out the Door." You can then check students' work and then return their work and go over the answers at the beginning of the next class period.

Daily Math Warm-Ups includes many elements that will help students master a wide range of mathematical concepts. These include:

- 180 five-problem lessons based on standards specified by the National Council of Teachers of Mathematics

- 18 multiple-choice assessment tests in standardized-test format, to help identify concepts mastered and concepts in need of reteaching

- 12 real-world application extension activities

- A reproducible problem-solving strategy guide for students (on the inside back cover)

- Plenty of computation, graph, and word-problem solving opportunities that become more difficult as students progress through the school year

Lesson 1

1. Donetta has 214,589 buttons. If her grandmother gives her 2,000 more buttons, how many buttons does she now have? How do you know? Write a number sentence, solve the problem, and explain your answer.

_____

_____

_____

2. $7 \times 6 =$

3. $9 \div 3 =$

4. $8 \times 11 =$

5. Use the following number to complete the chart.
567,891,243

What Numeral Is in the . . .	
One thousands place?	
Hundred thousands place?	
Tens place?	
Hundred millions place?	
Ones place?	
Ten thousands place?	
One millions place?	
Hundreds place?	
Ten millions place?	

Lesson 2

1. What is the value of the 4 in 231,498,239?

_____

2. $8 \times 8 =$

3. $6 \div 2 =$

4. $12 \times 6 =$

5. Use the following number to complete the chart.
426,809,135

What Numeral Is in the . . .	
One thousands place?	
Hundred thousands place?	
Tens place?	
Hundred millions place?	
Ones place?	
Ten thousands place?	
One millions place?	
Hundreds place?	
Ten millions place?	

Lesson 3

1. A nursing home recorded the number of cards received each day. On Monday, the center received 4,218 cards. On Tuesday, it received 1,000 cards. On Friday, it received 3,000 cards. How many cards did the center receive on all 3 days combined?

_____

2. $8 \times 2 =$

3. $12 \times 11 =$

4. $10 \div 2 =$

5. Use the following number to complete the chart.
578,093,145

What Numeral Is in the . . .	
One thousands place?	
Hundred thousands place?	
Tens place?	
Hundred millions place?	
Ones place?	
Ten thousands place?	
One millions place?	
Hundreds place?	
Ten millions place?	

Lesson 4

1. What is the place value of the 6 in the number 867,923,145?

_____

2. $6 \times 7 =$

3. $9 \times 8 =$

4. $10 \div 5 =$

5. Use the following number to complete the chart.
820,145,693

What Numeral Is in the . . .	
One thousands place?	
Hundred thousands place?	
Tens place?	
Hundred millions place?	
Ones place?	
Ten thousands place?	
One millions place?	
Hundreds place?	
Ten millions place?	

Lesson 5

1. Lewis collects bubble gum wrappers. When he was 8 years old, he collected 1,594 wrappers. When he was 9 years old, he collected 2,000 wrappers. When he was 10 years old, he collected 3,000 wrappers. How many wrappers did he collect in all 3 years combined?

_____

2. $7 \div 1 =$

3. $8 \times 5 =$

4. $7 \times 10 =$

5. Use the following number to complete the chart.
560,821,345

What Numeral Is in the . . .	
One thousands place?	
Hundred thousands place?	
Tens place?	
Hundred millions place?	
Ones place?	
Ten thousands place?	
One millions place?	
Hundreds place?	
Ten millions place?	

Lesson 6

1. Graham collects sports cards. If he has 989 cards in one set, 2,997 cards in a second set, and 12,001 cards in a third set, estimate about how many cards Graham has. Circle the letter beside the best estimate.

   A. 15,000 cards   B. 17,000 cards   C. 16,000 cards   D. 9,000 cards

2. $3 \times 9 =$

3. $8 \times 7 =$

4. $6 \div 3 =$

5. Using the information in the chart, write the number in the blank below.

_____

Place Value	Number
One thousands place	6
Hundred thousands place	9
Tens place	1
Hundred millions place	5
Ones place	7
Ten thousands place	2
One millions place	4
Hundreds place	8
Ten millions place	3

Lesson 7

1. Mrs. Mackay put candy in 4 bags for a math lesson. If she put 316 candies in one bag, 798 candies in another bag, 899 candies in a third bag, and 889 candies in a fourth bag, about how many thousand candies does she have?

   _____

2. $9 \times 6 =$

3. $12 \div 4 =$

4. $11 \times 5 =$

5. Using the information in the chart, write the number in the blank below.

   _____

Place Value	Number
One thousands place	6
Hundred thousands place	8
Tens place	0
Hundred millions place	9
Ones place	6
Ten thousands place	3
One millions place	1
Hundreds place	3
Ten millions place	0

Lesson 8

1. If Michael has 790 paper clips, Marcel has 987 paper clips, and Ming has 210 paper clips, about how many thousand paper clips do the 3 friends have altogether?

   _____

2. $9 \times 9 =$

3. $9 \div 9 =$

4. $12 \times 7 =$

5. Using the information in the chart, write the number in the blank below.

   _____

Place Value	Number
One thousands place	3
Hundred thousands place	5
Tens place	7
Hundred millions place	9
Ones place	8
Ten thousands place	6
One millions place	4
Hundreds place	2
Ten millions place	1

Name _____

Lesson 9

1. Mr. Ramos wants his students to read books that are at least 400 pages in length. The books he chose have 589 pages, 894 pages, 400 pages, and 899 pages. About how many thousand pages are in all of the books combined?

_____

2. 9 x 3 =

3. 7 x 8 =

4. 8 x 6 =

5. Using the information in the chart, write the number in the blank below.

Place Value	Number
One thousands place	1
Hundred thousands place	8
Tens place	4
Hundred millions place	6
Ones place	3
Ten thousands place	9
One millions place	0
Hundreds place	4
Ten millions place	2

_____

Lesson 10

1. The Cookie Cutter Company makes chocolate chip cookies. Last week it made 5,009 cookies on Monday, 12,900 cookies on Tuesday, and 6,021 cookies on Wednesday. About how many thousand cookies did the company make during those 3 days?

_____

2. 9 x 5 =

3. 7 x 7 =

4. 8 x 12 =

5. Using the information in the chart, write the number in the blank below.

Place Value	Number
One thousands place	6
Hundred thousands place	4
Tens place	8
Hundred millions place	0
Ones place	7
Ten thousands place	5
One millions place	7
Hundreds place	5
Ten millions place	9

_____

Lesson 11

1. Write the number in expanded form. 625,087,435

_____

2. The graph below represents the number of pages Jessica read each week for 2 months. How many books would you predict she read in Week 8? Why?

_____

_____

3. 2 x 7 =

4. 8 ÷ 2 =

5. 9 x 4 =

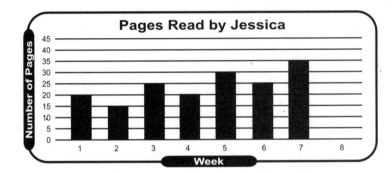

Lesson 12

1. Write the number in expanded form. 874,093,301

_____

2. The table shows the number of candy bars consumed by a group of friends. Based on the information given, how many candy bars do you think they will eat in Week 8? Why?

_____

_____

_____

3. 6 x 11 =

4. 12 ÷ 3 =

5. 12 x 12 =

Candy Bars Consumed

Week	Candy Bars
1	37
2	41
3	40
4	44
5	43
6	47
7	46
8	?

Lesson 13

1. 9 x 4 =

2. 8 x 8 =

3. 8 x 6 =

4. Write the expanded number in standard form.
    700,000,000 + 4,000,000 + 10,000 + 6,000 + 30 + 8

    _____

5. Fill in the blanks to complete the pattern, and write the rule.
    2   6   4   8   6   10   _____   _____   _____

    _____

    _____

Lesson 14

1. Write the number in word form.   890,258,003

    _____

    _____

2. 9 x 9 =

3. 6 x 8 =

4. 5 x 9 =

5. Fill in the blanks to complete the pattern.

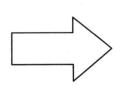  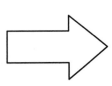    _____   _____

                                       Daily Math Warm-Ups Grade 5

Lesson 15

1. 6 x 9 =

2. 7 x 7 =

3. 5 x 6 =

4. Write the number in expanded form. 409,294,006

    _____

5. Fill in the blanks to complete the pattern, and write the rule.

    8 10 12 _____ _____

    _____

Lesson 16

1. Write the number in expanded form. 490,628,071

    _____

2. 8 x 4 =

3. 5 x 8 =

4. 4 x 9 =

5. Based on the temperatures for the week, if the pattern continues, would you predict a warmer or cooler day on Sunday? Why?

    _____

    _____

    _____

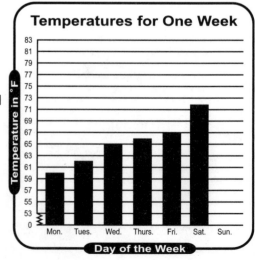

Name _____

Lesson 17

1. 9 x 7 =

2. 4 x 8 =

3. 8 x 8 =

4. Write the number in standard form.
   400,000,000 + 60,000,000 + 900,000 + 10,000 + 300 + 1

   _____

5. Fill in the blanks to complete the pattern, and write the rule.

   4   7   ☆   10   13   ☆   16   19   ☆   _____   _____

Lesson 18

1. Write the number in word form. 456,093,302

   _____

2. 7 x 9 =

3. 7 x 7 =

4. 3 x 4 =

5. Look at the table. Based on the pattern, what would the water temperature be on Saturday? Explain.

   _____

   _____

   _____

Water Temperature	
Day	**Temperature in ˚F**
Monday	68˚
Tuesday	70˚
Wednesday	72˚
Thursday	74˚
Friday	76˚
Saturday	?

Lesson 19

1. Write the number in standard form.
   four hundred three million, five hundred fifty-eight thousand, seven

   _____

2. 9 x 10 =

3. 8 x 3 =

4. 12 x 9 =

5. Fill in the blanks to complete the pattern, and write the rule.

   520   1,040   2,080   _____   _____

   _____

   _____

Lesson 20

1. 7 x 10 =

2. 24 ÷ 6 =

3. 81 ÷ 9 =

4. Write the number in expanded form. 843,902,002

   _____

5. Fill in the blanks to complete the pattern, and write the rule.

   20   60   50   150   140   _____   _____   _____

   _____

   _____

Lesson 21

1. Marco and Andy went to the mall on Saturday to purchase backpacks. They each had $50.00. The backpacks cost $29.95 each. About how much money total will the boys have left after they purchase 2 backpacks?

   _____

2. 5 x 9 =

3. 6 x 4 =

4. 4 x 7 =

5. According to the line graph, how many backpacks will be sold on Saturday, if the pattern continues? Why?

   _____

   _____

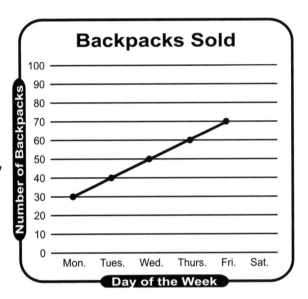

Backpacks Sold

Lesson 22

1. If Carly pays $9.89 for a pair of sunglasses and gives the cashier $20.00, how much money will she receive in change?

   _____

2. 28 ÷ 7 =

3. 12 x 4 =

4. 18 ÷ 3 =

5. Look at the pattern below. What will the 10th shape be?

   _____

Lesson 23

1. Nicolas and Tamara each spent $5.50 at the arcade. They gave the cashier $20.00 for their combined purchases. How much total change should they receive?

_____

2. $35 \div 7 =$

3. $6 \times 6 =$

4. $15 \div 3 =$

5. Jim is selling tickets to a play. He has sold tickets for the last 10 days. If the pattern continues, how many tickets can he plan to sell on Day 11?

_____

Tickets Jim Sold	
Day	Number of Tickets
1	6
2	7
3	9
4	12
5	16
6	21
7	27
8	34
9	42
10	51

Lesson 24

1. $64 \div 8 =$

2. $11 \times 12 =$

3. $54 \div 6 =$

4. Christopher and Nina mowed yards to earn money last summer. They each earned $10.00 per yard, and they each mowed 10 yards. How much money did they earn altogether?

_____

5. Christopher and Nina decided to put some of their money in the bank. They put $20 each in the bank. It will earn them $0.50 per month in interest. In 6 months, how much interest will they earn together?

_____

Lesson 25

1. Pat and Holly want to go to the movies. If tickets cost $6.50 each and snacks cost $5.00 each, how much money will they need altogether?

    _____

2. 6 x 9 =

3. 7 x 4 =

4. 9 x 9 =

5. Look at the chart. Do you predict that the temperature will be warm enough to wear shorts on Friday? Why or why not?

Temperature Chart	
Day	**Temperature in ˚F**
Monday	75˚
Tuesday	80˚
Wednesday	85˚
Thursday	90˚
Friday	

Lesson 26

1. If the pattern of shapes below continues, what will the 6th shape be?

           _____

2. 40 x 5 =

3. 200 x 6 =

4. 6 x 80 =

5. Look at the line graph. What is the best estimate of the number of families watching television on all 4 days at 8:00 P.M.?

    A. 80,000
    B. 90,000
    C. 70,000
    D. 100,000

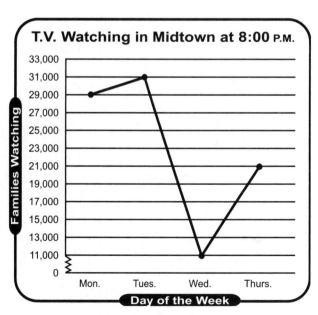

T.V. Watching in Midtown at 8:00 P.M.

Lesson 27

1. Look at the shapes. Which shape does not belong? Why?

  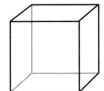

_____

2. 5 x 50 =

3. 6 x 400 =

4. 80 x 3 =

5. Look at the table to the right. About how many people shopped at Fast Foods Monday through Saturday?

_____

Shoppers at Fast Foods	
Day	Number of Shoppers
Monday	2,890
Tuesday	9,020
Wednesday	10,001
Thursday	13,890
Friday	15,000
Saturday	20,980

Lesson 28

1. Look at the shapes. Which shape does not belong? Why?

_____

2. 7 x 50 =

3. 400 x 3 =

4. 20 x 6 =

5. Look at the numbers. If the pattern continues, what will the 12th number be? 8, 7, 12, 11, 16, 15, 20, 19 . . . _____

18

Lesson 29

1. 8 x 20 =

2. 50 x 5 =

3. 800 x 4 =

4. Look at the numbers. Which one does not belong? Explain your answer.

    55   9   84   57   _____

    _____

5. Look at the pattern. What will the 15th item be? _____

    5   10 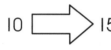 15   20   25   30 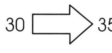 35   40

Lesson 30

1. Think about the numbers 30, 55, 77, and 99.
    Which number does not belong? _____ Explain your answer.

    _____

    _____

2. Based on the following data, what is the best estimate of the number of people who visited Mossville Elementary School last week?

    _____

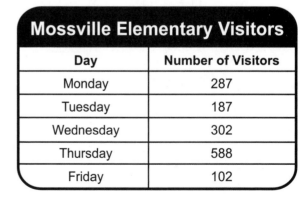

Mossville Elementary Visitors	
Day	**Number of Visitors**
Monday	287
Tuesday	187
Wednesday	302
Thursday	588
Friday	102

3. 9 x 10 =

4. 30 x 6 =

5. 7 x 300 =

Lesson 31

1. Plot the following coordinates on the coordinate plane. Then, connect the points. What polygon have you created?
(1,2) (2,4) (4,4) (5,2)

_____

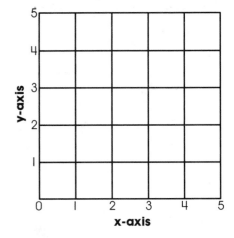

2. 70 x 80 =

3. 500 x 20 =

4. 60 x 30 =

5. Use the graph to determine how many hours Emily spent watching television. Explain your answer.

_____

_____

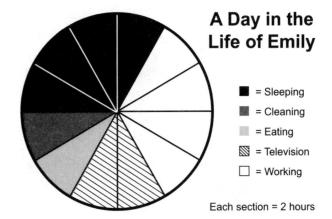

A Day in the Life of Emily

■ = Sleeping
■ = Cleaning
▨ = Eating
▨ = Television
□ = Working

Each section = 2 hours

Lesson 32

1. Andrew sleeps 8 hours each day. If he goes to school for 7 hours, does chores for 2 hours, and does homework for $1\frac{1}{2}$ hours, how many hours does he have left in a day? _____

2. 50 x 70 =

3. 300 x 30 =

4. 80 x 20 =

5. Plot the following coordinates on the coordinate plane. Then, connect the points. What polygon have you created?
(3,3) (3,6) (6,6) (6,3)

_____

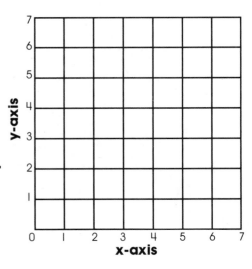

Lesson 33

1. Lisa worked 3 hours a day for 4 days last week, 2 hours a day for 3 days this week, and she will work $3\frac{1}{2}$ hours a day for 2 days next week. How many hours will she have worked in all 3 weeks combined?

_____

2. 5 x 80 =

3. 40 x 900 =

4. 40 x 4 =

5. Plot the following coordinates on the coordinate plane. Then, connect the points. What polygon have you created?
(3,5)   (5,8)   (7,5)   (5,2)

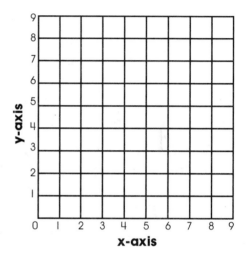

_____

Lesson 34

1. Tashina has to be at school at 7:30 A.M. She got up at 6:00 A.M. If it took her 45 minutes to get ready, 30 minutes to eat, and 20 minutes to walk from home to school, did she arrive on time? Why or why not?

_____

2. 60 x 6 =

3. 50 x 200 =

4. 30 x 70 =

5. Plot the following coordinates on the coordinate plane. Then, connect the points. What polygon have you created?
(3,1)   (3,8)   (7,8)   (7,1)

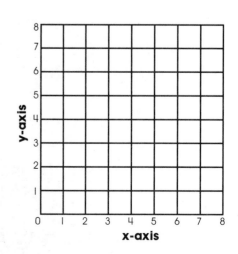

_____

Lesson 35

1. Arnie kept a log of how long he slept. Based on the data, how long might he expect to sleep on Night 8?

   _____

2. 20 x 70 =

3. 300 x 90 =

4. 30 x 80 =

5. Plot the following coordinates on the coordinate plane. Then, connect the points. What polygon have you created?
   (1,4)   (4,8)   (8,8)   (5,4)

   _____

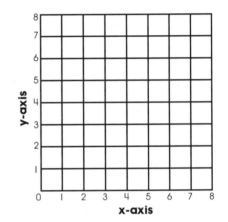

Arnie's Sleep Log	
Night	Time Slept
1	7 hours, 10 minutes
2	7 hours, 35 minutes
3	8 hours
4	8 hours, 25 minutes
5	8 hours, 50 minutes
6	9 hours, 15 minutes
7	9 hours, 40 minutes
8	

Lesson 36

1. Maria has $40.00. Based on the information in the bar graph, does Maria have enough money to cover her expenses?

   _____

2. 2,000 x 30 =

3. 55 ÷ 5 =

4. 80 ÷ 8 =

5. If the rectangle on the coordinate grid were turned one-quarter turn clockwise on the (1,2) coordinate, what would its other coordinates be?

   _____

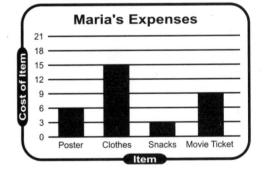

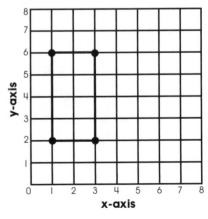

Lesson 37

1. If the triangle on the coordinate grid were turned one-quarter turn clockwise on the (2,4) coordinate, what would its other coordinates be?

   _____

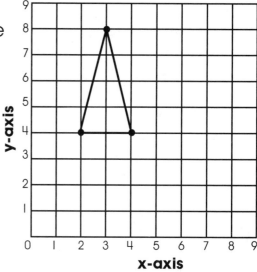

2. 3,000 x 40 =

3. 88 ÷ 8 =

4. 60 ÷ 5 =

5. Susan wants to purchase some school supplies. She will buy 3 packs of paper at $0.75 per pack, 8 pencils at $0.50 per pack of 2 pencils, and a backpack for $15.00. How much will she spend on school supplies in all?

   _____

Lesson 38

1. Donisha's new blouse costs $15.85. If she gives the cashier $20.00, how much change will she receive?

   _____

2. 4,000 ÷ 20 =

3. 800 x 20 =

4. 90 ÷ 3 =

5. If the triangle on the coordinate grid were reflected upside-down, what would its coordinates be?

   _____

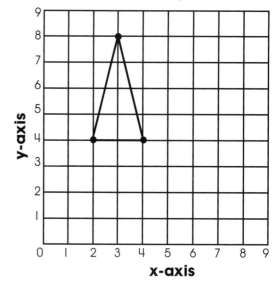

Lesson 39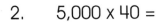

1. Danielle saved her paycheck. If she puts $40.00 in the bank, and it earns $1.50 interest each month for 10 months, how much interest will she have earned? _____

2. 5,000 x 40 =

3. 99 ÷ 9 =

4. 20 x 30 =

5. Look at the triangle on the coordinate grid. If it were moved so that its bottom, left vertex was coordinate (5,4), what would its other coordinates be?

    _____

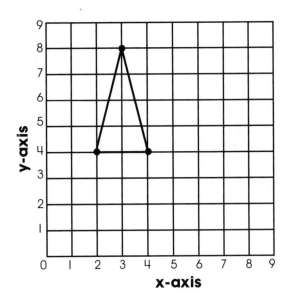

Lesson 40

1. Macala's twin brothers have a birthday tomorrow. She bought each of them stuffed animals for $12.50 each, including tax. If she gave the cashier $30.00, how much change did she receive?

    _____

2. Look at the triangle on the coordinate grid. If it were moved so that its bottom, right vertex was coordinate (9,4), what would its other coordinates be?

    _____

3. 2,000 x 50 =

4. 110 ÷ 10 =

5. 800 x 20 =

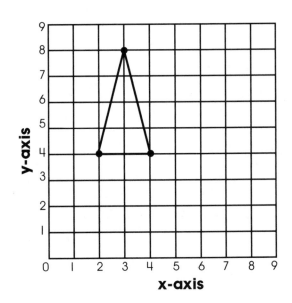

Lesson 41

1. Tabitha has eaten $\frac{1}{4}$ of her candy bar. Marco has eaten $\frac{2}{8}$ of his candy bar. Who has eaten the greater amount? Explain your answer.

2. $150 \times 3 =$

3. $366 \div 3 =$

4. $40,000 \div 10 =$

5. Look at the fractional representations. Which 2 rectangles show equivalent fractions? How do you know?

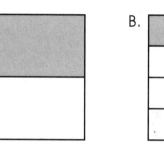
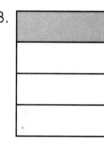
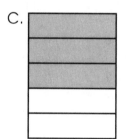
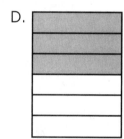

Lesson 42

1. $3 \times 400 =$

2. $2,500 \times 3 =$

3. $688 \div 2 =$

4. $60,000 \div 20 =$

5. Look at fractional representations A, B, and C. Different fractions have been shaded. Circle the letter beside the largest fraction.

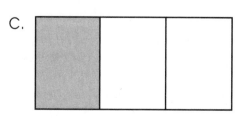
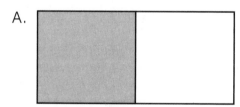
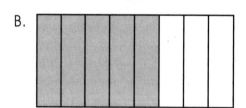

Daily Math Warm-Ups Grade 5

Lesson 43

1. $822 \div 2 =$

2. $50,000 \times 40 =$

3. $600,000 \div 3 =$

4. Tina and Ramón each ate $\frac{1}{3}$ of their pizza. Liza and Tom each ate $\frac{1}{4}$ of their pizza. Who ate more pizza: Tina and Ramón, or Liza and Tom?

_____

5. Look at the following fractional representations. Draw an X on the 2 circles that show a set of equivalent fractions.

Lesson 44

1. $530 \times 2 =$

2. $466 \div 2 =$

3. $700,000 \div 10 =$

4. $840,000 \div 4 =$

5. Look at the pictures of fractions. Put the letters of the rectangles in order to show the shaded fractions from least to greatest.

_____

A. 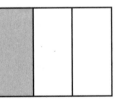   B.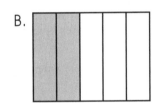

C.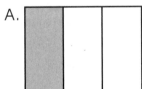

D. 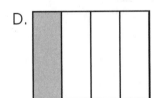   E.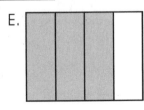

Lesson 45

1. $1,000,000 \times 60 =$

2. $684 \div 2 =$

3. $822 \div 2 =$

4. Martin has a candy bar made up of 12 small squares. If he has to share it equally with his brother and sister, how many pieces will each receive?

_____

5. Circle the letter of the fraction picture equivalent to $\frac{6}{8}$.

A.   B.   C.   D.

Lesson 46

1. Circle the letter beside the diagram that shows a pattern, or net, that you might use to build a tent with a pointed top.

   A.

2. $5,000 \times 0.03 =$

3. $4,500 \div 100$

4. $25 \times 0.2 =$

5. What is the range of the data in the line graph?

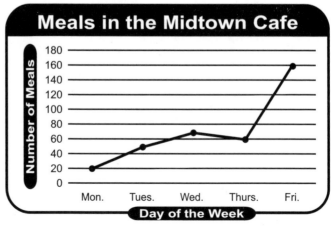

Meals in the Midtown Cafe

_____

Lesson 47

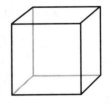

1. How many square faces make up a cube?

   _____

2. 15 x 0.2 =

3. 6,000 x 0.04 =

4. 6,800 ÷ 2 =

5. Carl's grades for daily work in mathematics for the last 4 days are 80, 90, 95, and 100. What is the range of his grades?

   _____

Lesson 48

1. The chart shows the rainfall in Mira, Mississippi last week. What is the range of the data?

   _____

2. 350 x 0.01 =

3. 1,500 x 0.02 =

4. 57,000 ÷ 100 =

5. How many rectangle faces make up a rectangular prism?

   _____

Rainfall in Mira, MS	
Day of Week	Rainfall
Monday	5 cm
Tuesday	8.2 cm
Wednesday	2 cm
Thursday	9 cm
Friday	4.5 cm
Saturday	3.9 cm
Sunday	2.1 cm

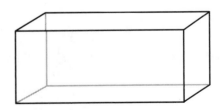

Lesson 49

1. How many pentagon and triangle faces make up a pentagonal pyramid?

_____

2. 33,000 x 0.03 =

3. 84,000,000 ÷ 1,000 =

4. 86,000 ÷ 20 =

5. Last Tuesday, 450 students ate lunch in the cafeteria. The frequency chart shows how many students in each grade ate lunch. What is the range of the numbers?

Students in Cafeteria	
Grade Level	Number of Students
1	80
2	110
3	175
4	25
5	60

_____

Lesson 50

1. How many rectangle and pentagon faces make up a pentagonal prism?

_____

2. 75 x 0.02 =

3. 7,000 x 0.003 =

4. 6,800 ÷ 40 =

5. Corinna's teacher assigned a class project. Corinna counted mailboxes on 6 streets in her neighborhood. The following frequency table shows Corinna's data.

   What is the range of the numbers?

Corinna's Mailbox Count	
Street Name	Number of Mailboxes
Apple Tart Street	8
Pear Tree Lane	12
Celery Station	6
Grape Way	21
Plum Court	9
Carrot Avenue	15

_____

Lesson 51

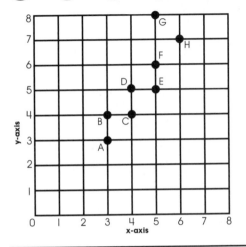

Key

A= Mark's Home   E= Shelf Shoes
B= Library   F= Molly's Antiques
C= City Hall   G= Evie's Emporium
D= Green's Cleaners H= Dale's Diner

1. Use the coordinate grid to answer the problem: Mark left home and went to the library. His next stop was City Hall. Green's Cleaners was his third stop. Next, he took some shoes to Shelf Shoes. If he continues this pattern, where will Mark go next?

   _____

   What are the building's coordinates?

   _____

2. Fill in the blank to complete the pattern of fractions.

   $\frac{1}{2}$ $\frac{2}{4}$ $\frac{3}{6}$ $\frac{4}{8}$ _____

3. $6,000 \div 0.20 =$

4. $\frac{4}{5} = \frac{n}{10}$ n = _____

5. $4.5 \times 20 =$

Lesson 52

1. Circle the letter of the picture showing the equivalent of $\frac{4}{5}$.

2. If each face of a cube is 4 square centimeters, what is the surface area of the cube?

   _____

A.   B.   C.

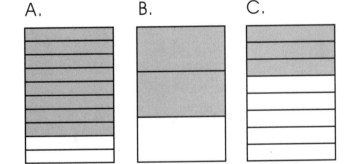

3. $4,500 \div 0.03 =$

4. $\frac{2}{3} = \frac{8}{n}$ n = _____

5. $5.2 \times 30 =$

Lesson 53

1. Look at the following pattern, or net. If you folded the net, what 3-dimensional figure would you have? What would the surface area of the 3-dimensional figure be if each square equals 1 square unit?

_____

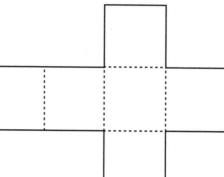

2. $80,000 \div 0.04 =$

3. $8.1 \times 0.1 =$

4. $\dfrac{3}{n} = \dfrac{9}{12}$ n = _____

5. If rectangles equal $0.50 and squares equal $0.25, what is the value of a rectangular prism?

_____

Lesson 54

1. $40.2 \times 0.1 =$

2. $900,000 \div 3 =$

3. $\dfrac{14}{21} = \dfrac{2}{n}$ n = _____

4. Look at the pattern of fractions. Fill in the blank.

$\dfrac{24}{48}$ $\dfrac{12}{24}$ $\dfrac{6}{12}$ _____

5. If a triangle is worth $1.00 and a pentagon is worth $3.00, what is the value of a pentagonal pyramid?

_____

Lesson 55

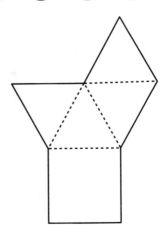

1. Look at the pattern, or net. When folded, what 3-dimensional figure is created?

   _____

2. $80.01 \times 0.1 =$

3. $\dfrac{9}{n} = \dfrac{3}{4}$ $n =$ _____

4. $660,000 \div 0.30 =$

5. Noah is building a square house. He wants the base of the roof and the top of the house to match exactly. What 3-dimensional figure might he place on top of the house to create the roof?

   _____

Lesson 56

1. If the arrow were rotated one-quarter to the right, what would it look like? Draw it in the box.

2. Write the standard representation for the number.
   $600,000,000 + 50,000,000 + 20,000 + 1,000 + 80 + 5$ _____

3. What is the average of the following numbers? 25, 10, 50, 100, 15

   _____

4. $5,000 \times 0.003 =$

5. The table shows 5 friends' race times. List the girls' names in the order that they finished the race.

   _____

   _____

Race Times	
Team Member	**Time**
Dena	6.45 seconds
Mia	8.98 seconds
Damara	9.45 seconds
Stephie	4.65 seconds
Erin	4.56 seconds

Lesson 57

1. What is the average of the following numbers? 40, 60, 55, 45, 100

    _____

2. 89,000 x 0.0001 =

3. Write the number in word form. 988,203,001

    _____

    _____

4. Put the following numbers in order from least to greatest.
   2.01   9.21   2.19   9.12

    _____

5. If the figure were flipped top to bottom, what would it look like? Draw it in the box.

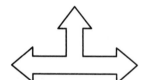 

Lesson 58

1. Write the number in expanded form. 800,431,030

    _____

2. 999,000 ÷ 9 =

3. 250,000 x 0.03 =

4. Put the following numbers in order from greatest to least.
   1.3   0.59   5.09   0.95

    _____

5. If the figure were rotated one-quarter turn to the left, what would it look like? Draw it in the box.

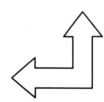 

Lesson 59

1. 112,000 x 0.004 =

2. Write the number in standard form.
   ten million, four hundred twelve thousand, five hundred six

   _____

3. Put the following numbers in order from greatest to least.
   7.09   0.99   9.79   7.99

   _____

4. What is the average of the following set of numbers?
   35, 65, 99, 25, 101, 25, 0

   _____

5. If the figure were rotated one-quarter turn to the
   left, what would it look like? Draw it in the box.

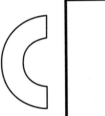 

Lesson 60

1. Write the number in expanded form. 89,092,003

   _____

2. What is the average of the following numbers? 59, 21, 30, 67, 100, 23

   _____

3. Put the numbers in order from least to greatest. 3.03   3.3   0.333   1.03

   _____

4. 36,000 x 0.001 =

5. If the following shape were rotated
   one-quarter turn to the right, what
   would it look like? Draw it in the box.

 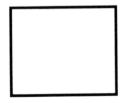

Lesson 61

1. Sam wants to pack some candies into a box with a volume of 1.5 cubic meters. Each candy has a volume of 1 cubic centimeter. How many candies will fit in the box? _____

2. $1.5 \times (2 \times 5) =$

3. $65,000 \times 0.01 =$

4. $(3 \times 2) + 4 =$

5. Look at the line graph. What will Saturday's temperature be? Why?

_____

_____

_____

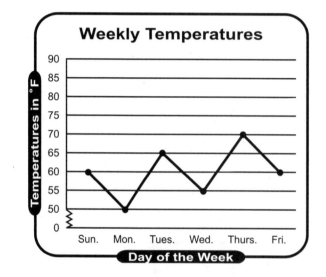

Lesson 62

1. Look at the chart showing the cost of a certain pair of shoes over the last 5 years. How much will the same pair of shoes cost in Year 6? Why?

_____

_____

_____

2. $3.5 \times (1 \times 100) =$

3. $98,000 \times 0.001 =$

4. $(9 \times 8) - 12 =$

Cost of Shoes	
Year	Cost
1	$29
2	$38
3	$47
4	$56
5	$65
6	

5. How many cubes with a volume of 2 cubic centimeters will fit into a larger cube with a volume of 8 cubic centimeters?

_____

Lesson 63

1.   80 − (4 x 20) =

2.   (1.5 x 200) ÷ 10 =

3.   12.01 x 0.2 =

4.   How many cubic centimeters are there in a rectangular prism with a volume of 12 cubic meters?

     _____

5.   Complete the following pattern, then write the rule.
     $4.05 $40.50 $405.00   _____

     _____

Lesson 64

1.   (5.5 x 10) + 25 =

2.   1.1 + (3 x 6) =

3.   84,000 ÷ 0.02 =

4.   Complete the following pattern, then write the rule.
     $93 $89.50 $86 $82.50   _____

     _____

5.   If twelve 1 cm^3 cubes will fill the bottom of a box that is 10 cm high, how many 1 cm^3 cubes will it take to fill the entire box?

     _____

Lesson 65

1. (1.5 x 30) x 2 =

2. 3.5 + (20 x 3) =

3. 99,000 ÷ 0.3 =

4. Complete the following pattern, then write the rule.
   $100 $300 $600 $800   _____

   _____

5. If the bottom of a rectangular box will hold twenty 1 cm^3 cubes and the box is 40 centimeters high, will the box hold 1 cubic meter? How do you know?

   _____

Lesson 66

1. $\frac{2}{8} + \frac{3}{8} =$

2. 0.25 x 1,000 =

3. Tara wants to install a fence around her garden. If the garden is 8 feet long and 6 feet wide, how many feet of fencing will Tara need to buy?

   _____

4. What is another way to write 4 x 4 x 4 x 4 using exponential notation?

   _____

5. Look at the stem and leaf chart showing Carla's grades. Estimate her average score. Explain your answer.

Carla's Grades			
5	0	0	
8	7	8	9
9	3	7	9
10	0	0	

   _____

   _____

Daily Math Warm-Ups Grade 5

Lesson 67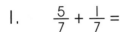

1. $\frac{5}{7} + \frac{1}{7} =$

2. $\frac{2}{9} + \frac{2}{9} =$

3. $2,000 \times 0.25 =$

4. Marcia wants to put a wallpaper border around her room. The room is 12 feet long and 10 feet wide. How many feet of wallpaper border does Marcia need to buy?

    _____

5. What is the average of the following numbers?
    88   42   0   12   8   30

    _____

Lesson 68

1. $\frac{5}{12} + \frac{6}{12} =$

2. $\frac{4}{5} - \frac{1}{5} =$

3. $0.3 \times 400,000 =$

4. What is the average of the following numbers?
    8.5   2   1.5   90   8

    _____

5. Look at the square. What is the perimeter of the square?

    _____

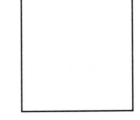

5 inches

Lesson 69

1. If I side of a square is 8 yards long, what is the perimeter of the square?

   _____

2. $\frac{7}{20} - \frac{4}{20} =$

3. 4,200 x 0.002 =

4. $\frac{8}{15} + \frac{3}{15} =$

5. The stem and leaf chart shows the number of soft drinks consumed by 10 customers at Largo's Grocery. What is the average number of soft drinks consumed by these 10 customers?

   _____

Soft Drinks Consumed			
1	0	0	
2	5	5	
3	5		
4	0	0	
5	0	0	0

Lesson 70

1. What is the average of the following numbers?
   2.5   0   8.5   9   20

   _____

2. 80,000 x 0.04 =

3. $\frac{4}{12} + \frac{1}{12} =$

4. $\frac{8}{21} - \frac{2}{21} =$

5. Look at the figure. What is the perimeter of the figure in centimeters?

   _____

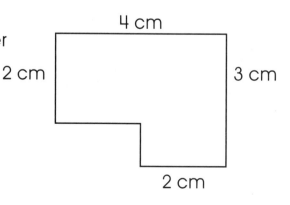

4 cm

2 cm   3 cm

2 cm

Lesson 71

1. Nell wants to measure the diameter of a circle. If the distance from a point on the circumference of the circle to the midpoint is 8 feet, what is the diameter of the circle?

   _____

2. $1.2 \times 0.3 =$

3. $\frac{1}{6} + \frac{4}{6} =$

4. $5^2 + 2^3 =$

5. Look at the Venn Diagram. Place the following numbers.

   15, 50, 45, 30, 36

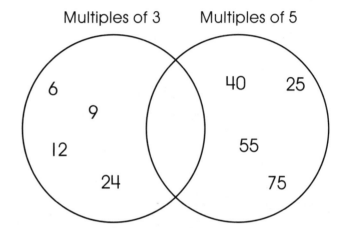

Multiples of 3   Multiples of 5

6   9   40   25

12   55

24   75

Lesson 72

1. $3^3 \times 2^2 =$

2. $3.2 \times 0.2 =$

3. $\frac{6}{10} + \frac{3}{10} =$

4. List the common multiples of 3 and 4, through 24.

   _____

5. If Marquisa has a trampoline with a diameter of 18 feet, what is the radius of the trampoline? _____ How do you know?

   _____

   _____

Lesson 73

1. $5^2 - 2^3 =$

2. $5.01 \times 0.02 =$

3. If Doug is eating a pizza with a diameter of 12 inches and Trudy has a pizza with a diameter 3 times the radius of Doug's pizza, what is the diameter of Trudy's pizza?

   _____

4. List the common multiples of 2 and 5, through 40.

   _____

5. $\dfrac{7}{10} - \dfrac{2}{10} =$

Lesson 74

1. $8^2 + 5^2 =$

2. $10.02 \times 0.04 =$

3. Kasahito's backyard is a circular space with an area of 11.5 feet. He wants to install a swimming pool with a diameter of 25 feet in the backyard. Is it possible? Why or why not?

   _____

   _____

4. $\dfrac{23}{25} - \dfrac{5}{25} =$

5. List the common multiples of 6 and 9, through 54.

   _____

Lesson 75

1. $22.2 \times 0.003 =$

2. $9^2 - 3^2 =$

3. Tony is creating circles for a project. His teacher wants a circle with a diameter of 2.5 inches. She also wants a circle with a diameter 5 times the radius of the first circle. What is the diameter of the second circle?

    _____

4. List the common multiples of 7 and 3, through 35.

    _____

5. $\frac{18}{19} - \frac{14}{19} =$

Lesson 76

1. Khalid has $150 in his pocket. He wants to purchase 12 CDs for $9.98 each, including tax. About how much is his total purchase? Does he have enough money?

    _____

2. $\frac{2}{3} = \frac{6}{n}$ $n =$ _____

3. $1.2 \times 0.1 =$

4. $\frac{5}{9} - \frac{2}{9} =$

5. Look at the graph. If the store owner wants to purchase more candy, but can only buy one kind, which brand would you suggest he buy? Why?

    _____

    _____

    _____

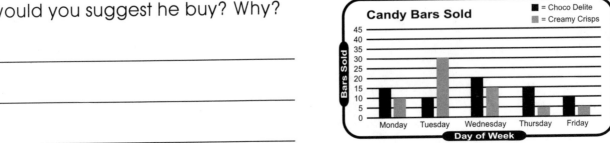

Lesson 77

1. $\frac{8}{n} = \frac{24}{48}$ n = _____

2. 9.03 x 0.001 =

3. $\frac{9}{12} - \frac{4}{12} =$

4. Nana wants to purchase a toy for her grandson. The toy costs $20.50 including tax. If Nana has $15.00 plus 12 quarters and 21 dimes, does she have enough money to purchase the toy? _____

5. Mr. Jeffers owns a flower shop. He is trying to decide whether to buy lilies or marigolds. He buys each flower at the same price. Last week, he sold 10 lilies at $5.00 each and 8 marigolds at $6.50 each. If he can sell the same number of each flower at the same price this week, which flower should he purchase? Why?

Lesson 78

1. Look at the frequency chart. It shows the 3 top selling brands at Barry's Bicycle Shop. If Barry wants to order more bikes, but can only afford to order 1 brand, which should he order? Why?

Barry's Bicycle Shop Sales			
Bike Brand	Number Sold	Barry's Cost	Customer's Cost
Wheeler Dealer	10	$50	$75
Cross Country	20	$60	$80
Dream Maker	30	$50	$60

2. 3.5 x 0.002 =

3. $\frac{8}{12} - \frac{3}{12} =$

4. $\frac{6}{12} = \frac{2}{n}$ n = _____

5. Fill in the blanks to complete the pattern.
    $20.00 $22.50 $25.00 $27.50   _____   _____   _____

Lesson 79

1. $2.3 \times 0.002 =$

2. $\dfrac{6}{20} - \dfrac{3}{20} =$

3. $\dfrac{9}{15} = \dfrac{3}{n}$ n = _____

4. Odessa wants to order lunch. She has $5.00. If hamburgers are $3.50, french fries are $1.25, and drinks are $1.50, does Odessa have enough money to buy them all? How do you know?

   _____

5. Fill in the blanks to complete the following pattern. Then, write the rule.
   7   14   11   22   19   _____   _____   _____

   _____

Lesson 80

1. $10.1 \times 0.001 =$

2. $\dfrac{8}{19} - \dfrac{3}{19} =$

3. $\dfrac{4}{8} = \dfrac{n}{2}$ n = _____

4. Fill in the blanks to complete the following pattern. Then, write the rule.
   3   9   10   30   31   _____   _____

   _____

5. Justin needs his bike repaired. It will cost $30. To earn the money, he will mow yards. He earns $8 for every yard he mows. How many yards will Justin have to mow to earn enough money to pay for his bike repair? How do you know?

   _____

   _____

Lesson 81

1. Logan wants to seat 8 people for dinner this evening. If she has 3 square card tables, how might she arrange seating so that everyone is seated beside another person and all of the tables are used?

    _____

    _____

2. 3.5 x 0.2 =

3. 6.5 ÷ 0.5 =

4. $\frac{8}{15} - \frac{3}{15} =$

5. Look at the chart. Put the boys in order from least to greatest distance walked.

Distance Walked	
Boy's Name	**Distance**
Chris	3 meters
Bryson	4,500 centimeters
Moe	2.9 meters
Harold	3,500 centimeters
José	3.2 meters

    _____

Lesson 82

1. Kristin is having a party. She has invited 8 people. She has 4 square tables. How might Kristin arrange seating so that everyone is seated next to another person and all of the tables are used?

    _____

    _____

2. 9.5 x 0.001 =

3. 9.3 ÷ 0.3 =

4. $\frac{8}{20} - \frac{5}{20} =$

5. Mrs. Kinlaw wants to take a picture of her 4 sons standing in order from shortest to tallest. Fill in the chart, ranking the boys first, second, third, or fourth.

Mrs. Kinlaw's Sons' Heights		
Son's Name	**Height**	**Order by Height**
Mark	4.5 feet	
Raphael	5.4 feet	
Dennis	3.2 feet	
Roberto	5.1 feet	

Lesson 83

1. $\frac{6}{15} + \frac{5}{15} =$

2. $8.9 \times 0.01 =$

3. $7.2 \div 0.8 =$

4. Ron is planning a surprise birthday party for his wife. He has invited 8 other people. He has 4 tables. How can he seat everyone, including himself and his wife, so that each person is seated next to another person and all 4 of the tables are used?

   _____

   _____

5. Ms. John's class took a timed test. Below are the times of 4 students. Rank the students in order from the first to the last to finish.
   Mick: 2.5 minutes; Dan: 3.2 minutes; Rick: 2.3 minutes; Jon: 3.5 minutes

   _____

Lesson 84

1. Angelica has 5 square tables. What is the largest number of people she can seat if all of the tables are placed together end-to-end?

   _____

2. $8.1 \div 0.9 =$

3. $5.3 \times 0.2 =$

4. $\frac{5}{6} - \frac{3}{6} =$

5. The table shows the number of miles run by cross-country team members. In the table, fill in the blanks to put the team members in order by distances run, from the least to the greatest distance.

Miles Run	
Team Member	**Miles**
_____ Marcia	8.2
_____ Joan	7.02
_____ Mia	8.05
_____ Tina	7.15
_____ Mabel	8

Lesson 85

1. $\frac{9}{20} - \frac{3}{20} =$

2. $6.1 \times 0.3 =$

3. $8.5 \div 0.5 =$

4. What is the greatest number of people you can seat at four 4-person tables if everyone is seated beside another person?

   _____

5. Put the following numbers in order from greatest to least.
   8.5   9.2   3.1   1.03   9.04   8.09

Lesson 86

1. $0.25 = \frac{n}{4}$ $n =$ _____

2. $\frac{9}{14} - \frac{7}{14} =$

3. $45 \div 0.9 =$

4. Ann Marie has 4 pieces of red candy, 6 pieces of yellow candy, and 4 pieces of orange candy in a bag. Which color of candy will she most likely pull out first, if she puts her hand into the bag without looking? Why?

   _____

   _____

5. Look at the number line. Circle the letter representing 3.7.

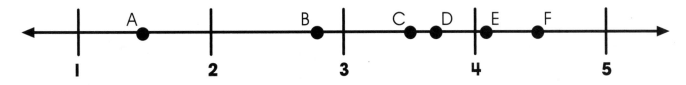

Lesson 87

1. If Barney has 12 yellow markers, 6 blue markers, and 4 red markers in a bag, and he pulls one out without looking, which color is he most likely to choose? Why?

    _____

2. $\frac{8}{16} - \frac{4}{16} =$

3. $64 \div 0.8 =$

4. $0.10 = \frac{1}{n}$ $n =$ _____

5. Look at the number line. Circle the letter representing 2.8.

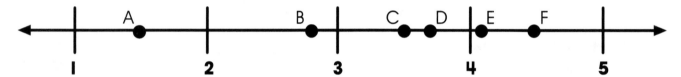

Lesson 88

1. Pressley has 5 blue pencils, 6 red pencils, and 4 orange pencils in her desk drawer. What color pencil is she least likely to pick out if she chooses one without looking? Why?

    _____

2. $\frac{4}{5} - \frac{2}{5} =$

3. $7.5 \div 0.05 =$

4. $0.50 = \frac{n}{2}$ $n =$ _____

5. Look at the number line. Circle the letter representing 1.5.

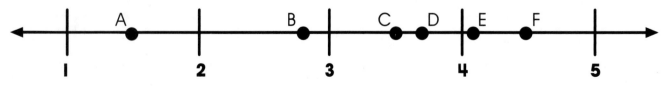

Lesson 89

1. Monty has shuffled 10 cards. He asks Dana to choose a card without looking. If Monty has 4 tens, 2 ones, 3 fives, and 1 seven, which card is Dana most likely to pick first? Why?

   _____

2. $8 \div 0.05 =$

3. $\dfrac{18}{20} - \dfrac{5}{20} =$

4. $\dfrac{45}{50} = \dfrac{n}{10}$ $n =$ _____

5. Look at the number line. Circle the letter representing 4.5.

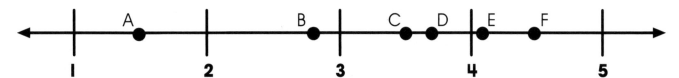

Lesson 90

1. Nikki is setting the table for her mother. In the silverware drawer, there are 7 forks, 9 spoons, and 8 knives. If she takes out a piece of silverware without looking, what item is she least likely to take out first? Why?

   _____

2. $\dfrac{6}{18} + \dfrac{3}{18} =$

3. $9 \div 0.03 =$

4. $0.75 = \dfrac{3}{n}$ $n =$ _____

5. Look at the number line. Circle the letter representing 4.1.

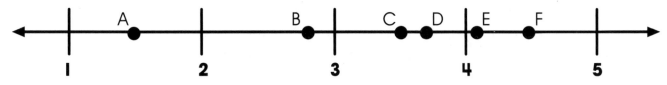

Daily Math Warm-Ups Grade 5

Lesson 91

1. Amy has a total of $4.25 in her purse. She has 4 dollars and 5 coins. What coins does she have in her purse?

_____

2. $5.2 \times 0.2 =$

3. $30,000 \times 0.5 =$

4. $2\frac{1}{4} + 3\frac{1}{4} =$

5. What is the average number of pages in the books Sarah read?

Pages Read by Sarah	
Book	**Pages Read**
1	250
2	500
3	250
4	450
5	200

_____

Lesson 92

1. $2\frac{1}{3} + 3\frac{1}{3} =$

2. $6.1 \times 0.02 =$

3. $4,000 \times 0.6 =$

4. If Nina has 1 dollar and 12 coins for a total of $2.26, what coins might Nina have?

_____

5. Mrs. Macon is the cafeteria manager. The table shows Mrs. Macon's bread order for the last 4 months. What is the average number of loaves that Mrs. Macon buys each month?

Mrs. Macon's Bread Order	
Month	**Number of Loaves**
October	650
November	700
December	600
January	850

_____

Lesson 93

1. Sheryn wants to buy earrings that cost $5.20. If she has 2 dollars, 7 quarters and 21 dimes, does she have enough money?

    _____

2. 2.5 x 0.03 =

3. 0.5 x 15,000 =

4. $11 \frac{3}{5} + 9 \frac{1}{5} =$

5. What is the average of the following numbers?
    60   150   200   40   50

    _____

Lesson 94

1. The stem and leaf table shows Dina's grades for this semester. If a "B" is between 80 and 90, did Dina make a B this semester? Why or why not?

    _____

    _____

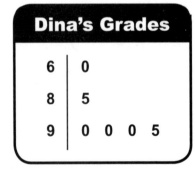

2. $20 \frac{2}{3} - 15 \frac{1}{3} =$

3. 0.3 x 1.3 =

4. 60,000 x 0.3 =

5. Timmy's mom gave him his allowance in coins this month. She gave him 13 quarters, 18 dimes, and 20 nickels. If Timmy receives $6.00 allowance each month, did he receive the correct amount of money?

    _____

Lesson 95

1. $9 \times 0.06 =$

2. $10\frac{1}{4} + 21\frac{2}{4} =$

3. $40{,}000 \times 0.2 =$

4. Kenya found 3 quarters, 6 dimes, 5 nickels, and 2 pennies in the bottom of her purse. How much money does she have?

   _____

5. Find the average of the numbers.
   25, 60, 75, 40, 80

   _____

Lesson 96

1. $10.5 \times 0.2 =$

2. $1\frac{1}{7} + 2\frac{3}{7} =$

3. $\frac{7}{8} - \frac{3}{8} =$

4. Brian and Bill are selling tickets to the school play. If Brian sells 1 ticket every 20 minutes, and Bill sells 2 tickets every 30 minutes, who will sell the most tickets after 5 hours?

   _____

5. Look at the T-chart. What operation is being performed on the numbers in the Input column in order to get the numbers in the Output column?

   _____

Input	Output
3	12
4	16
5	20
N	_____

Lesson 97

1. If Stephanie runs 2 miles in 3 hours and Mark runs 3 miles in 4 hours, who will run farther in 12 hours?

   _____

2. $0.3 \times 9.1 =$

3. $4\frac{5}{8} - 2\frac{4}{8} =$

4. $\frac{9}{12} - \frac{6}{12} =$

5. Look at the T-chart. What operation is being performed on the numbers in the Input column in order to get the numbers in the Output column?

Input	Output
14	12
13	11
12	10
N	____

   _____

Lesson 98

1. $\frac{4}{6} - \frac{2}{6} =$

2. $6\frac{1}{4} + 7\frac{2}{4} =$

3. $10 \times 0.04 =$

4. Lucas earns $10.00 every 2 hours for mowing yards. Ben earns $15.00 every 4 hours for mowing yards. Who will earn $30.00 first? Why?

   _____

   _____

5. Fill in the blank to complete the T-chart.

Input	Output
6	30
7	35
8	40
N	____

Lesson 99

1. Martina can read 20 pages in 30 minutes. Arcella can read 30 pages in 40 minutes. Who could read 100 pages first? Why?

_____

_____

2. $0.2 \times 4 =$

3. $8\frac{6}{9} - 5\frac{1}{9} =$

4. $1\frac{4}{11} + 3\frac{6}{11} =$

5. Fill in the blank to complete the T-chart.

Input	Output
6	18
7	21
8	24
N	_____

Lesson 100

1. Complete the following pattern, then write the rule.
   2, 1, 5, 4, 20, 19, _____, _____

2. Fill in the blank to complete the T-chart.

3. $2{,}000 \times 0.03 =$

4. $2\frac{7}{8} - 1\frac{1}{8} =$

5. $4\frac{6}{10} - 2\frac{3}{10} =$

Input	Output
20	15
21	16
22	17
N	_____

Lesson 101

1. 460,000,000 ÷ 230 =

2. $\frac{1}{4}$ x 20 =

3. 0.25 x 400 =

4. Abby is creating a design on her kitchen floor using an isosceles triangle. She knows that the 2 base angles of the triangle equal 110°. What is the measurement of the third angle of the triangle?

    _____

5. Roberto is creating a patterned border for his son's playroom. What will the 10th shape look like if the pattern below continues? In the box, draw the 10th shape.

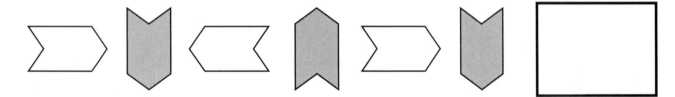

Lesson 102

1. 660,000,000 ÷ 300 =

2. $\frac{1}{3}$ x 60 =

3. 0.11 x 300 =

4. What is the sum of all of the angles of a rectangle? _____

5. Fill in the blanks to complete the pattern below.

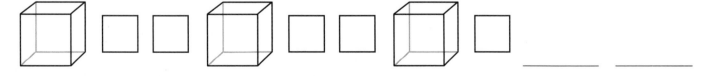

Lesson 103

1. 86,000,000 ÷ 430 =

2. $\frac{1}{9}$ x 72 =

3. 0.12 x 400 =

4. What is the sum of all of the angles of a square? _____

5. Look at the following pattern. If it continues, what will the 9th shape look like? Draw it in the box below.

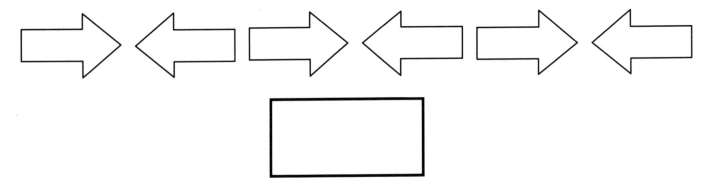

Lesson 104

1. 90,000,000 ÷ 300 =

2. $\frac{1}{5}$ x 25 =

3. 0.05 x 150 =

4. If the sum of 2 angles of a triangle is 150°, what is the measurement of the third angle? _____

5. Fill in the blanks to complete the pattern.

 2  3  4  ____ ____

Lesson 105

1. $160,000,000 \div 4,000 =$

2. $\frac{1}{3} \times 21 =$

3. $0.6 \times 6,000 =$

4. If the sum of 3 angles of a quadrilateral is 270°, what is the measurement of the 4th angle? _____

5. Look at the following pattern. If it continues, what will the 9th shape look like? Draw the 9th shape in the box below.

Lesson 106

1. $\frac{1}{3} \times n = 4$ n = ____

2. $5\frac{1}{4} + \frac{4}{4} =$

3. $8\frac{7}{8} - 4\frac{3}{8} =$

4. Ernie poured 2 liters of water into a red bucket. He poured 1,500 milliliters of water into a blue bucket. Which bucket has the most water?

_____

5. Continue the pattern to complete the chart.

Number of Keys on the Key Ring					
Number of Keys	3	5	7	9		
Number of Key Rings	1	2	3	4		

Lesson 107

1. $\frac{1}{2} \times 50 = n$ $n =$ _____

2. $6\frac{1}{2} + \frac{2}{2} =$

3. $9\frac{8}{10} - 4\frac{4}{10} =$

4. Mary's mother is baking a cake. She needs $\frac{1}{2}$ liter of milk. If she has 500 milliliters of milk, does she have enough? Why or why not?

_____

5. Continue the pattern to complete the recipe chart.

Nutty Bar Recipe Chart						
Cups of Nuts	$\frac{1}{2}$	1	$1\frac{1}{2}$	2		
Number of Recipes	1	2	3	4		

Lesson 108

1. A road crew is painting a stripe down the middle of a road. The stripe they are painting is $4\frac{1}{2}$ meters long. They have enough paint for a stripe 500 centimeters long. Do they have enough paint? Why or why not?

_____

2. $\frac{1}{4} \times n = 3$ $n =$ _____

3. $8\frac{2}{5} + \frac{5}{5} =$

4. $9\frac{8}{12} - 2\frac{7}{12} =$

5. Fill in the blanks to complete the pattern.

3	5	7	9	___	___
9	15	21	27	___	___

Lesson 109

1. $\frac{1}{8} \times 32 = n$ $n = $ _____

2. $12\frac{4}{6} + \frac{6}{6} = $

3. Bob has $\frac{1}{4}$ liter of soda in his cup. How many milliliters are in his cup?

   _____

4. $12\frac{5}{8} - \frac{1}{8} = $

5. Fill in the blank to complete the T-chart.

Input	Output
4	10
5	11
6	12
N	_____

Lesson 110

1. $\frac{1}{6} \times n = 6$ $n = $ _____

2. $9\frac{2}{3} + \frac{3}{3} = $

3. $9\frac{4}{5} - 2\frac{4}{5} = $

4. How many meters equal 650 centimeters?

   _____ meters

5. Fill in the blanks to complete the pattern.

4	8	12	16	___	___
8	16	24	32	___	___

Lesson 111

1. What is the value of "n" in the following equation? $(4 \times 5) \div 5 = n^2$

   n = _____

2. $10.5 \times 0.01 =$

3. $\dfrac{6}{5} - \dfrac{2}{5} =$

4. Greg is filling a large food bin with grain. The bin holds 12 kilograms. Greg can carry 4,000 grams of grain in his bucket. How many times will Greg have to empty his bucket into the food bin to fill it up?

   _____ times

5. Tasha uses 2 bags of chocolate chips to make 4 dozen cookies. How many bags of chocolate chips will she need to make 10 dozen cookies? Complete the pattern in the chart, then fill in the blank below.

   Tasha's Cookie Recipe

Bags of Chocolate Chips	2	4	6	8	10
Dozens of Cookies	4	8			

   Tasha will need _____ bags of chocolate chips.

Lesson 112

1. If $(3 + n) \times 5 = 25$, what is the value of "n"?

   n = _____

2. $5.5 \times 0.05 =$

3. $\dfrac{9}{7} - \dfrac{2}{7} =$

4. If Dino's cup holds $\dfrac{1}{2}$ liter, how many times would he need to fill the cup to have 500 milliliters?

   _____ times

5. Fill in the blanks to complete the pattern.

5	10	15	___	___
9	14	19	___	___

Lesson 113

1. If $(5 \times 6) - n = 10$, what is "n"?

    n = _____

2. $\frac{8}{6} - \frac{4}{6} =$

3. $20.3 \times 0.001 =$

4. How many grams are equal to 3 kilograms?

    _____ grams

5. Fill in the blanks to complete the pattern.

1	5	25	___	___
2	10	50	___	___

Lesson 114

1. If $8 \times (n + 3) = 72$, what is "n"?

    n = _____

2. $20.2 \times 0.003 =$

3. $\frac{10}{6} - \frac{4}{6} =$

4. How many centimeters are in $10 \frac{1}{2}$ meters?

    _____ centimeters

5. Fill in the blanks to complete the pattern.

50	48	46	___	___
25	24	23	___	___

Lesson 115

1. If $5 \times 6 + (2 \times n) = 34$, what is "n"?

   n = _____

2. $50.1 \times 0.02 =$

3. $\frac{6}{3} - \frac{4}{3} =$

4. How many centimeters are in 12 meters?

   _____ centimeters

5. Fill in the blanks to complete the pattern.

60	50	40	___	___
6	5	4	___	___

Lesson 116

1. Mrs. Norton is organizing a field trip. She is using vans that can carry 6 people each. If she has 2 classes of 20 students each and all of the students must leave at the same time, how many vans will she need to transport both classes?

   _____ vans

2. $8 \times (2 + 5) = (2 + 5) \times n$

   n = _____

3. $\frac{1}{5} \times 10 =$

4. $4 \times (8 \div 2) = n^2$

   n = _____

5. Look at the circle graph. How many hours did David spend sleeping?

   _____ hours

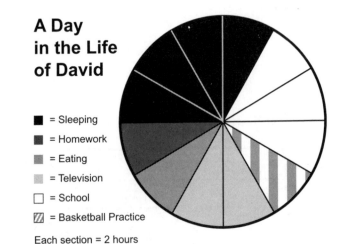

A Day in the Life of David

- ■ = Sleeping
- ■ = Homework
- ■ = Eating
- ▨ = Television
- □ = School
- ▨ = Basketball Practice

Each section = 2 hours

Lesson 117

1. If 3 x (2 + 5) = n, what is the value of "n"?
   n = _____

2. If 2 x (5 + 5) = 5 x n, what is the value of "n"?
   n = _____

3. $\frac{1}{3}$ x 30 =

4. There are 55 students in Mr. Brower's class. How many tables does he need in order to seat all of his students, if each table seats 4 students?

   _____ tables

5. If 25 discs fit in a box, how many boxes will Bart need for 260 discs?

   _____ boxes

Lesson 118

1. If (4 + 2) x n = 15 + n, what is the value of "n"?
   n = _____

2. If (20 – 5) + n = 5 x 5, what is the value of "n"?
   n = _____

3. $\frac{2}{3}$ x 9 =

Use the circle graph to answer questions 4 and 5.

4. What fraction of the time did Andy spend watching movies?

   _____

5. What fraction of the time did Andy spend watching cartoons?

   _____

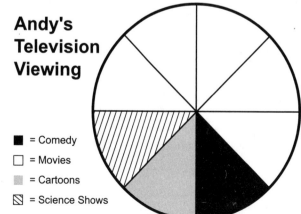

Andy's Television Viewing

■ = Comedy
□ = Movies
▨ = Cartoons
▨ = Science Shows

Lesson 119

1. If $14 \times (1 \times 1) = n + 7$, what is the value of "n"?

   n = _____

2. If $35 - (5 \times 2) = n$, what is the value of "n"?

   n = _____

3. $\frac{4}{5} \times 40 =$

4. How many drinks will fit in 20 drink boxes if 25 drinks fit in one drink box?

   _____ drinks

5. Emily has an hour to get from her house to her grandmother's house. If she drives $\frac{1}{4}$ of the way in 14 minutes and continues at the same speed, will she arrive in less than an hour? Explain your answer.

   _____

   _____

Lesson 120

1. If $2 + (9 \times 2) = 10 + n$, what is the value of "n"?

   n = _____

2. If $19 - (2 \times 3) = 10 + n$, what is the value of "n"?

   n = _____

3. $\frac{2}{4} \times 16 =$

4. $\frac{5}{6} \times 30 =$

5. Rob and Karen are organizing a car pool to go to the lake. They can fit 5 people in each car. If 24 people are going to the lake, how many cars do they need?

   _____ cars

Lesson 121

1. Look at the numbers below. Circle the number that has a smaller digit in the thousands place than in the ten millions place.

    321,092,512   932,402,387   425,933,021

2. $\frac{1}{6}$ x 48 =

3. $\frac{8}{5} + \frac{2}{5}$ =

4. Eugene wants to create a garden with an area of 9 square feet. What is the largest perimeter he can create if he may only create a square or a rectangle? Explain your answer.

    _____

    _____

5. Look at the figure. What are the lengths of line segments A and B, if the center line segment forms a line of symmetry?

    A = _____   B = _____

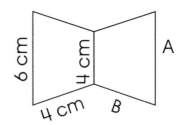

Lesson 122

1. Look at the numbers below. Circle the number with the smallest digit in the ten thousands place.

    230,984   942,009   518,390   849,420

2. Give your solution as a mixed number. $\frac{9}{7} + \frac{1}{7}$ =

3. What is the perimeter of the triangle?

    _____ centimeters

    6 cm

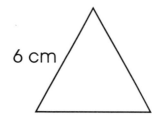

4. $\frac{1}{7}$ x 49 =

5. What is the perimeter of a square with 8-inch sides? _____ inches

Lesson 123

1. Look at the numbers below. Circle the number with the smallest digit in the millions place.

    249,982,039   294,838,951   198,928,391   248,958,185

2. $\frac{2}{8}$ x 16 =

3. Give your solution as a mixed number. $\frac{8}{5} + \frac{4}{5}$ =

4. What is the perimeter of an equilateral triangle with one edge equal to 12 meters?

    _____

5. What is the perimeter of the rectangle?

    8 in.

    7 in.

Lesson 124

1. Look at the numbers below. Circle the number that has the largest digit in the ten millions place.

    839,294,099   256,938,291   389,392,928   390,293,342

2. $\frac{4}{6}$ x 12 =

3. Give your solution as a mixed number. $\frac{9}{11} + \frac{15}{11}$ =

4. What is the measure of each side of an equilateral triangle with a perimeter of 24 meters?

    _____

5. What is the measure of each side of a square with a perimeter of 60 inches?

    _____

Lesson 125

1. Look at the numbers below. Circle the number that has the largest digit in the hundred thousands place.

873,483,903   9,301,091   32,093,192   83,293,294

2. $\frac{3}{6} \times 90 =$

3. Give your solution as a mixed number. $\frac{4}{8} + \frac{10}{8} =$

4. What is the perimeter of a rectangle that is 15 inches long and 10 inches high?

_____

5. If an isosceles triangle has 2 sides measuring 10 cm in length, what is the measure of its third side, if the perimeter of the triangle is 27 cm?

_____

Lesson 126

1. A page of Tina's scrapbook holds 399 stickers. She wants to fill 4 more pages. If the stickers are sold in sheets of 500, how many sheets of stickers will Tina need to buy in order to fill up 4 scrapbook pages?

_____

2. Circle the prime number. 9   51   27   17

3. What is "n" if $(5 + 3) \times n = 400$
   n = _____

4. $\frac{2}{8} \times 40 =$

5. Look at the graph. What is the difference in the range of 5th and 6th grade students eating in the cafeteria?

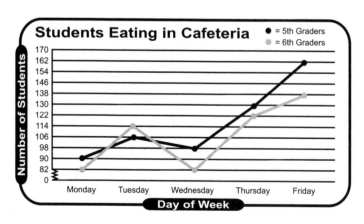

Lesson 127

1. Circle the composite number. 7   0   1   9

2. $\frac{3}{5} \times 15 =$

3. If $(4 \times 6) + 4 = n \times 7$, what is the value of "n"?   n = _____

4. If Mrs. Morehead feeds 2,000 students each day in the cafeteria and one can of beans feeds 20 students, how many cans of beans does she need to prepare each day?

    _____

5. What is the range of the following numbers?
    24, 99, 101, 93, 14, 104

    _____

Lesson 128

1. Circle the prime numbers. 7   5   13   15

2. If $2 \times 5 + (5 \times 2) = n \times 5$, what is the value of "n"?   n = _____

3. $\frac{2}{9} \times 18 =$

4. If Charlie has 1,500 magazines for sale and each person coming in the door purchases 5 magazines, how many people could possibly purchase magazines?

    _____

5. What is the range of the following numbers?
    99, 38, 29, 109, 294, 298, 18

    _____

Lesson 129

1. Circle the number that is not a prime number.

   1   5   17   23   99

2. If $(9 \times 3) + 3 = n \times 3$, what is the value of "n"?
   n = _____

3. $\frac{4}{7} \times 70 =$

4. Mr. and Mrs. Marks made 3 dozen cookies. If they have 4 children, how many cookies will each person get, including Mr. and Mrs. Marks?

   _____

5. What is the range of the following numbers?
   89, 29, 39, 499, 203, 488, 19

   _____

Lesson 130

1. Circle the number sentence that has a prime number solution.

   2 + 8 =   4 x 3 =   10 ÷ 2 =   10 – 6 =

2. $\frac{3}{8} \times 40 =$

3. If $(80 - 75) \times 2 = 8 + n$, what is the value of "n"?
   n = _____

4. Brantley is giving out 360 flyers at the mall. If he gives 3 fliers to each person he meets, to how many people can he give fliers?

   _____

5. What is the range of the following numbers?
   89, 293, 943, 29, 294, 43

   _____

Lesson 131

1. Write the decimal equivalent. $\frac{4}{5}$ =

2. What are the factors of 6? _____

3. Write the number in expanded form. 43,098,706

   _____

   _____

4. If Monique can fill candy boxes at a rate of 3 pieces every 2 minutes and Kenya can fill candy boxes at a rate of 5 pieces every 4 minutes, who will fill more boxes in 32 minutes?

   _____

5. Look at Bella's spinner.
   What number is she most likely to spin? _____

Lesson 132

1. Write the decimal equivalent. $\frac{5}{20}$ =

2. What are the factors of 10? _____

3. Write the number in standard form.
   300,000,000 + 3,000,000 + 4,000 + 200 + 1

   _____

4. Complete the pattern. 5, 10, 7, 14, 11, _____, _____, _____

5. Trish has 9 pieces of candy in a bag. If 4 pieces of candy are green, what are Trish's chances of pulling out a piece of candy that is not green, if she chooses without looking?

   _____

Lesson 133

1. Write the decimal equivalent. $\frac{4}{10}$ =

2. What are the factors of 25? _____

3. Write the number in word form. 29,301,002

_____

4. Complete the pattern.
2, 10, 12, 60, 62, _____, _____, _____

5. Sinclair has a box of 48 crayons. If 6 crayons are red, what are Sinclair's chances of pulling out a crayon that is not red, if he chooses a crayon without looking?

_____

Lesson 134

1. 0.40 = $\frac{4}{n}$ n = _____

2. What are the factors of 64? _____

3. Write the number in standard form.
four hundred five million, two hundred twenty-two thousand, three

_____

4. Complete the pattern.
5, 6, 12, 13, 26, _____, _____, _____

5. If Bryson has 5 action figures in a box and 2 of them are blue, what are his chances of picking an action figure out of the box that is not blue, if he chooses randomly?

_____

Lesson 135

1. Write the decimal equivalent. $\frac{5}{20} =$

2. What are the factors of 24? _____

3. Write the number in expanded form. 32,090,412

_____

Use the spinner to answer questions 4 and 5.

4. If Maryann spins the spinner, what are her chances of spinning a 2? _____

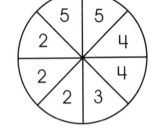

5. What two numbers does Maryann have an equal chance of spinning? _____ and _____

Lesson 136

1. What is the least common multiple of 3 and 4? _____

2. $\frac{2}{3} \times 15 =$

3. 0.9 x 100,000 =

4. A group of 7 students have qualified for a prize in Mrs. Warlick's class. The students are Raquel, Will, Terri, Tabitha, Carmen, Shaun, and Vincent. Mrs. Warlick will put their names in a hat and draw randomly. Names beginning with which letter have the best chance of winning the prize? Why?

_____

5. The line plot graph shows the scores of 10 people in Rhonda's class. What is the average score in this set of data?

_____

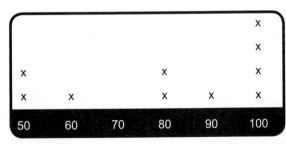

Lesson 137

1. What is the least common multiple of 10 and 15? _____

2. $\frac{4}{5} \times 80 =$

3. $0.8 \times 30,000 =$

4. Two spinners have 4 sections each. One of the spinners has 2 ones and 2 threes. The other spinner has 3 ones and 1 three. Which spinner is fair? How do you know?

   _____

5. Find the average of the following numbers. 150, 50, 200, 50, 100, 50

   _____

Lesson 138

1. What is the least common multiple of 7 and 9? _____

2. $\frac{1}{3} \times 99 =$

3. $40,000 \times 0.002 =$

Use the spinner to answer questions 4 and 5.

4. If Sherrie spins the spinner, what are her chances of spinning a 2 or a 3?

   _____

5. What are Sherrie's chances of spinning a 4 or a 5?

   _____

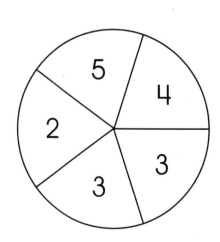

Lesson 139

1. What is the least common multiple of 8 and 6? _____

2. $\frac{2}{4}$ x 100 =

3. 0.05 x 150 =

Use the spinner to answer questions 4 and 5.

4. If Margo spins the spinner, what are her chances of spinning a 6?

    _____

5. If Margo spins a second time, what are her chances of spinning anything but a 6?

    _____

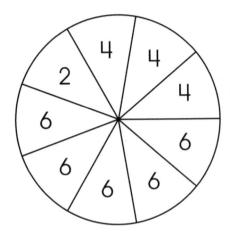

Lesson 140

1. What is the least common multiple of 10 and 12? _____

2. $\frac{3}{4}$ x 200 =

3. 160 x 0.0001 =

4. There are 24 students in Mrs. Dunn's homeroom. If $\frac{1}{4}$ of her students have names that begin with "S," what fraction of her students do not have names that begin with "S"?

    _____

5. Use information from #4 to help you answer this question: If Mrs. Dunn puts all 24 of her students' names in a hat and randomly draws a name, what are the chances that the name will begin with the letter "S"?

    _____

Lesson 141

1. $6 \times (4 + 4) \div 2^2 =$

2. What is the least common multiple of 6 and 4? _____

3. What are the factors of 32? _____

4. Tabitha has a box with a volume of 3.5 cubic liters. How many 1 centimeter cubes must she put in the box to fill it to capacity? _____

5. The graph shows how much time students spent watching TV last Monday. What is the mode of the data?

_____

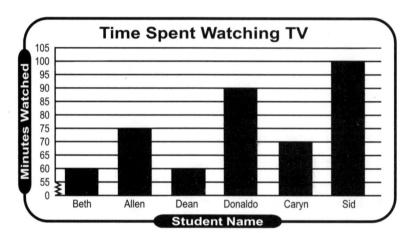

Time Spent Watching TV

Lesson 142

1. $4 \times (2 + 2) \div 2^2 =$

2. What is the least common multiple of 5 and 9? _____

3. What are the factors of 56? _____

4. How many cubic centimeters does it take to equal 1 cubic meter?

_____

5. What is the mode of the following set of numbers?
24, 94, 48, 24, 99, 102

_____

Lesson 143

1. $8 - (2 \times 2) + 9 =$

2. What are the common multiples of 4 and 9, through 108?

   _____

3. What are the factors of 51?

   _____

4. How many centimeters equal 5.5 meters?

   _____

5. What is the mode of the following set of numbers?
   88, 99, 111, 222, 88, 99, 88

   _____

Lesson 144

1. $9 \times (3 + 1) \times 3^2 =$

2. What are the common multiples of 2 and 5, through 30?

   _____

3. What are the factors of 28?

   _____

4. How many grams equal 1.5 kilograms?

   _____

5. What is the mode of the following set of numbers?
   22, 98, 58, 29, 49, 98, 88

   _____

Lesson 145

1. $4 \times (3 + 5) - 2^3 =$

2.   What is the least common multiple of 4 and 6? _____

3.   What are the factors of 45? _____

Use the data below to answer problems 4 and 5.

x				
x			x	
x			x	
x	x		x	
x	x	x	x	
Fiction	Nonfiction	Fairy Tales	Poetry	Each x = 4 students

4.   How many students are reading poetry? _____

5.   How many fewer students are reading nonfiction than fiction?
     _____

Lesson 146

1.   What is the least common multiple of 5 and 8? _____

2.   Jill ran 100 yards. Marty ran 299 feet. Who ran farther? How do you know?
     _____

3.   Which number is larger, $\frac{7}{4}$ or $1\frac{1}{2}$? _____

4. $5\frac{3}{4} - 2\frac{1}{4} =$

5.   Casey was the timekeeper at the last Hill High Race. Each runner's time is shown on the chart. Rank the runners from fastest to slowest time.

Race Times	
Opponent	**Time**
Chris	7.5 minutes
Miranda	$7\frac{1}{4}$ minutes
Damon	$8\frac{3}{4}$ minutes
Erika	8.5 minutes
Donica	6.5 minutes
Lario	8.0 minutes

_____

_____

Lesson 147

1. Which number is greater, $\frac{8}{5}$ or $1\frac{4}{5}$? _____

2. $6\frac{4}{5} - 1\frac{3}{5} =$

3. What is the least common multiple of 6 and 7? _____

4. Donley ran 450 yards in the race. Monica ran 1,400 feet. Who ran farther? How do you know?

   _____

5. Put the numbers in order from greatest to least.

   8.01   0.99   3.12   3.09   3.91

   _____

Lesson 148

1. Which number is greater, $\frac{9}{4}$ or $1\frac{3}{4}$? _____

2. $9\frac{3}{4} - 7\frac{1}{4} =$

3. What is the least common multiple of 5 and 12?

   _____

4. How many feet are in 15 yards?

   _____

5. Put the numbers in order from least to greatest.

   8.1   9.2   3.4   4.03   9.14

   _____

Lesson 149

1. Which number is greater, $\frac{8}{5}$ or $1\frac{1}{5}$? _____

2. $8\frac{7}{8} + 1\frac{1}{8} =$

3. What are the factors of 44?

   _____

4. How many yards are in 18 feet? _____

5. Put the numbers in order from least to greatest.

   2.03   3.04   4.90   4.8   2.1   3.2

   _____

Lesson 150

1. Which number is greater, $\frac{6}{5}$ or $1\frac{2}{5}$? _____

2. $8\frac{5}{6} - 3\frac{2}{6} =$

3. What are the factors of 23?

   _____

4. If Paulette ran 45 feet and Tanya ran 15 yards, who ran farther?

   _____

5. Put the numbers in order from greatest to least.

   10.4   4.01   4.25   10.09   5.3   5.90

   _____

Lesson 151

1. Circle the composite number. 7   19   51   5

2. $\frac{1}{7} \times 21 =$

3. $4,000,000 \times 0.02 =$

Use the chart to answer questions 4 and 5.

4. Look at the stem and leaf chart. What is the mode of the basketball scores? Is this more or less than an estimated average? How do you know?

Norton High Basketball Scores				
10	1	2	3	4
9	2	4	4	6	8
8	5	5	5	8

_____

5. The Norton High Basketball team has 1 more game to play. What score might you expect the team to get, based on the data in the chart? Why?

_____

Lesson 152

Use the table to answer questions 1 and 2.

Mr. Biggs' Class	
Month	**Number of Absences**
January	25
February	15
March	10
April	20
May	15

1. What is the average number of absences for all 5 months?

_____

2. What is the mode of the absences for all 5 months?

_____

3. Circle the number that is not a composite number. 33   21   45   17

4. $\frac{2}{3} \times 36 =$

5. $0.5 \times 6,000,000 =$

Lesson 153

1. Circle the composite number. 13   45   3   7

2. $\frac{5}{10}$ x 20 =

3. 12,000 x 0.3 =

4. What is the average of the following numbers? _____
   30   60   10   25   25

5. What is the mode of the following numbers? _____
   30   60   10   25   25

Lesson 154

1. Circle the prime number. 21   23   55   51

2. $\frac{2}{10}$ x 30 =

3. 0.04 x 60,000 =

Use the frequency chart to answer questions 4 and 5.

Cars Sold by Cary's Cars

Month	Number Sold
April	14
May	26
June	34
July	40
August	26

4. What was the average number of cars sold each month from April to August by Cary's Cars?

   _____

5. What is the mode of the frequency chart?

   _____

Name _____

Lesson 155

1. Circle the prime number. 75   99   101   19

2. $\frac{2}{8} \times 40 =$

3. $0.08 \times 100,000 =$

4. What is the range of the following numbers? _____
    41   58   92   85.6   91.2   12   112

5. What is the mode of the following numbers? _____
    32.1   44   94.1   32.1   59   93.1

Lesson 156

1. $\frac{2}{10} + \frac{4}{10} =$

2. $\frac{9}{16} - \frac{5}{16} =$

3. $6,000,000 \div 0.003 =$

4. Beth is reading a magazine that is 80 pages long. There are ads on every fourth page. If Beth opens the magazine to a random page, what are her chances of opening to a page with an ad on it?

    _____

5. The line graph shows Richie's sleep pattern over the last 6 days. If the pattern continues, how many hours do you think Richie will sleep on Saturday? Why?

    _____

    _____

    _____

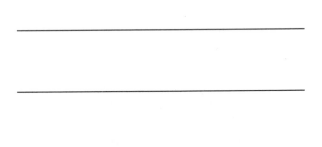

Richie's Sleep Pattern

Lesson 157

1. $\frac{8}{18} + \frac{2}{18} =$

2. $8\frac{7}{14} - \frac{2}{14} =$

3. $9{,}000{,}000 \div 0.003 =$

4. There were 9 pencils in Barry's pencil box. There were 4 blue pencils. If he chooses randomly, what are Barry's chances of choosing a color other than blue?

   _____

5. The frequency chart shows the number of cakes the Beruda Bakery baked over the last 4 weeks. Based on the data, how many cakes do you think they will bake in Week 5? Why?

   _____

   _____

   _____

Cakes Baked at Beruda Bakery	
Week	**Number of Cakes**
1	46
2	45
3	47
4	46
5	

Lesson 158

1. $\frac{9}{16} + 2\frac{1}{16} =$

2. $\frac{4}{5} + 8\frac{1}{5} =$

3. $2.5 \times 3{,}000 =$

4. Fill in the blanks to complete the pattern.
   $3.00 $4.50 $5.00 $6.50 $7.00   _____   _____

5. Juana's mom has forgotten where she put her favorite bowl. If there are 7 cabinets in the kitchen and her bowl is in one of them, what are her chances of finding the bowl in the first cabinet that she searches?

   _____

Lesson 159

1. $\frac{6}{12} + 2\frac{5}{12} =$

2. $9\frac{1}{2} - \frac{1}{2} =$

3. $9.1 \times 1,000,000 =$

4. Victor put 10 numbered cards in a cup. If 6 cards have odd numbers on them, what are Victor's chances of pulling out an even-numbered card, if he pulls out a card at random?

   _____

5. Fill in the blanks to complete the pattern.

   99   49.5   88   44   77   _____   _____

Lesson 160

1. $\frac{1}{5} \times 95 =$

2. $12\frac{3}{4} - \frac{1}{4} =$

3. $6\frac{8}{9} + \frac{4}{9} =$

4. Tina has a box containing 70 color photographs and 70 black-and-white photographs. If she chooses a photograph randomly from the box, what are her chances of choosing a color photograph?

   _____

5. Fill in the blanks to complete the pattern.

   98   89   87   78   _____   _____

Lesson 161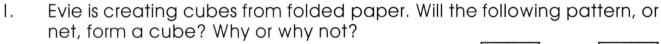

1. Evie is creating cubes from folded paper. Will the following pattern, or net, form a cube? Why or why not?

    _____

    _____

2. 45,000 x 0.002 =

3. $\frac{3}{8} + \frac{3}{8} =$

4. $\frac{9}{15} - \frac{4}{15} =$

5. What three-dimensional figures would be represented by the 2 sets of data on the chart below? Fill in the empty spaces to complete the chart.

Three-Dimensional Figure	Number of Faces	Number of Edges	Number of Vertices
	6	12	8
	6	10	6

Lesson 162

1. Look at the pattern, or net. Will it create a rectangular prism? Why or why not?

    _____

    _____

    _____

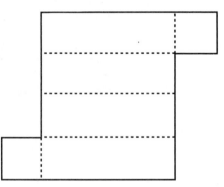

2. $\frac{4}{9} + \frac{2}{9} =$

3. $8\frac{4}{5} - 4\frac{1}{5} =$

4. 15,000 x 0.05 =

5. How many vertices does a cube have? _____

Lesson 163

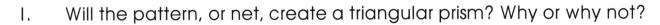

1. Will the pattern, or net, create a triangular prism? Why or why not?

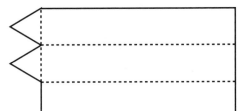

_____

_____

_____

2. $9\frac{1}{2} + 1\frac{1}{2} =$

3. $7\frac{5}{6} - \frac{2}{6} =$

4. $90 \times 0.003 =$

5. How many edges does a hexagonal prism have? _____

Lesson 164

1. Will the pattern, or net, create a cube? Why or why not?

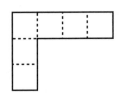

_____

_____

2. $8\frac{3}{4} - \frac{1}{4} =$

3. $15\frac{3}{5} + \frac{2}{5} =$

4. $40 \times 0.05 =$

5. Which figure has more edges, a square pyramid or a cube? Explain your answer.

_____

_____

Lesson 165

1. Will the pattern, or net, create a square pyramid? Why or why not?

   _____

   _____

2. $15\frac{1}{2} - \frac{1}{2} =$

3. $9\frac{3}{4} + 4\frac{1}{4} =$

4. $80,000 \div 0.2 =$

5. Which has more vertices, a rectangular prism or a cube? _____

Lesson 166

1. $45 \times 30 =$

2. Mary has to get to a baseball game by 7:00 P.M. It is now 5:30 P.M. If she snacks for 10 minutes, does homework for 35 minutes, cleans up for 40 minutes, and travels for 5 minutes, will she get to the game on time?

   _____

3. Order the following fractions from least to greatest. $\frac{1}{5}$ $\frac{1}{3}$ $\frac{1}{7}$ $\frac{1}{9}$ $\frac{1}{4}$

   _____

4. $1.5 \times 0.1 =$

5. Compare the table and the pictograph below. The book in the pictograph key equals how many books read?

   The book in the pictograph key equals _____ books read.

Books Read	
Month	**Books Read**
September	40
October	56
November	48
December	20

   Number of Books Read ☐ =

   Sept.
   Oct.
   Nov.
   Dec.

Lesson 167

1. 75 x 20 =

2. 2.5 x 0.2 =

3. Order the following fractions from least to greatest. $\frac{3}{10}$ $\frac{3}{9}$ $\frac{3}{5}$ $\frac{3}{4}$ $\frac{3}{12}$

_____

4. It is 5:50 P.M. If it takes Lori 15 minutes to drive home, can she stop by the grocery store for 20 minutes and be home at 6:25 P.M.? Why or why not?

_____

5. If Carlos creates a bar graph showing the number of homes in 10 large cities, should the numbers on his y-axis be scaled by 2s or 100s? Why?

_____

Lesson 168

1. 80 x 90,000 =

2. 0.2 x 2.04 =

3. Order the numbers from greatest to least. 4.5   1.2   1.02 $3\frac{1}{2}$ 5.4

_____

4. If Larry spends $\frac{1}{4}$ hour fixing a sandwich and $\frac{1}{2}$ hour eating it, how much time has passed in all? _____

5. Look at the frequency table and graph. Label the y-axis on the graph.

Temperature in °F	
Day	Temperature
Monday	80°
Tuesday	85°
Wednesday	70°
Thursday	75°
Friday	60°

Temperature in °F

Lesson 169

1. $210 \times 30 =$

2. $6.6 \times 0.001 =$

3. Order the following numbers from least to greatest.
$5\frac{1}{2}$ 4.6   9.05 $4\frac{1}{2}$ 9.5

_____

4. Which is larger, $\frac{5}{4}$ or $1\frac{1}{2}$? _____

5. Polly wants to clean her room before her friends arrive at 7:00 P.M. It is 4:45 P.M. How much time does she have to clean if she also needs 30 minutes to bathe?

_____

Lesson 170

1. $200 \times 300 =$

2. $2.7 \times 0.001 =$

3. Order the following fractions from least to greatest. $\frac{6}{8}$ $\frac{1}{2}$ $\frac{1}{4}$ $\frac{8}{8}$

_____

4. Abernathy's Apple Orchard has 50 trees that yield about 100 apples each. If he sells $\frac{1}{2}$ of his apples to a local grocery store, how many apples will he have left to sell at Mr. Abernathy's roadside stand?

_____

5. Deborah's teacher has asked her to create a display showing the temperature over a month's time. Which would best show the information: a stem and leaf chart, a line graph, or a pictograph? Why?

_____

_____

Lesson 171

1. $\frac{5}{6} \times 60 =$

2. $5.5 \times 1.01 =$

3. $\frac{6}{14} - \frac{4}{14} =$

4. Amir wants to get a playground ball from the P.E. cabinet. The cabinet contains 6 orange basketballs, 8 volleyballs, 4 green playground balls, and 8 orange playground balls. When Amir reaches into the cabinet, what are his chances of randomly picking out a playground ball first?

   _____

5. Look at the following data. In which week did Tina run at a constant speed?

   _____

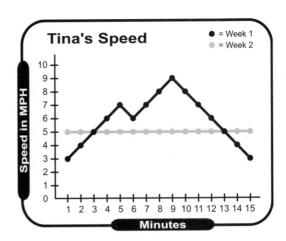

Lesson 172

1. $\frac{6}{7} \times 49 =$

2. $6.5 \times 0.01 =$

3. $\frac{6}{15} - \frac{3}{15} =$

4. If Meg spins a spinner that has the numbers 1 through 6 on it, what are the chances she will spin an odd number?

   _____

5. If Meg spins a spinner that has the numbers 1 through 6 on it, what are the chances she will spin a number less than 5?

   _____

Lesson 173

1. $\frac{9}{9} - \frac{7}{9} =$

2. $9.9 \div 0.03 =$

3. $18\frac{2}{5} - \frac{1}{5} =$

4. If Josh is running a race against 5 other equally skilled runners, what are his chances of winning?

   _____

5. If Andrew spins a spinner with the numbers 1 through 5 on it, what are his chances of not spinning an odd number?

   _____

Lesson 174

1. $8\frac{3}{12} - 1\frac{2}{12} =$

2. $81.9 \div 9 =$

3. $\frac{1}{6} \times 60 =$

Use the spinners below to answer questions 4 and 5.

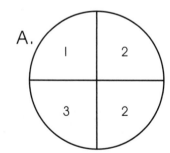
A.

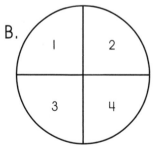
B.

4. Which spinner has equal odds? _____

5. Which spinner would you rather use if you were trying to spin a 2?

   _____

91

Lesson 175

1. $44\frac{1}{5} + 10\frac{2}{5} =$

2. $36.6 \div 0.03 =$

3. $\frac{1}{8} \times 16 =$

Use the frequency charts below to answer questions 4 and 5.

Fifth Grade Meals

Entrée	Number of Students
Pizza	120
Hamburgers	70
Hot Dogs	90
Tacos	80

Sixth Grade Meals

Entrée	Number of Students
Pizza	90
Hamburgers	40
Hot Dogs	100
Tacos	100

4. Who ate more meals, 5th graders or 6th graders? _____

5. If you were the cafeteria manager, which entrée would you serve most often, if you wanted students to eat in the cafeteria? _____

Lesson 176

1. Leah measured the perimeter of her bedroom for a border. If the length of the room is 10 meters and the width of the room is 8 meters, how many centimeters of border will she need to purchase? _____

2. What is the value of "n"? $(30 - 5) \div 5 + n = 10$
   n = _____

3. Look at the table. Which room in Kevin's house has the greatest area?

   _____

4. $1,500 \div 0.05 =$

5. $\frac{3}{5} \times 100 =$

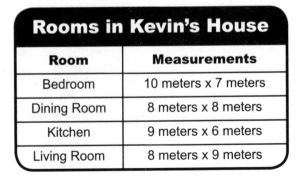

Rooms in Kevin's House

Room	Measurements
Bedroom	10 meters x 7 meters
Dining Room	8 meters x 8 meters
Kitchen	9 meters x 6 meters
Living Room	8 meters x 9 meters

Lesson 177

1. Look at the table. Which office space has the greatest perimeter?

   _____

2. $9.1 \times 0.001 =$

3. $\frac{5}{7} \times 28 =$

4. What is the value of "n"? $(50 \times 2) + 50 = n$

   n = _____

5. Sam wants to purchase $6\frac{1}{2}$ liters of paint for a charity building project. How many milliliters of paint does he need?

   _____

Office Space Measurements	
1	10 meters x 8 meters
2	9 meters x 11 meters
3	7 meters x 12 meters
4	8 meters x 9 meters

Lesson 178

1. Look at the table. Porchia has measured 4 rooms in her house. Which room has the smallest area?

   _____

2. $0.03 \times 3,600 =$

3. $\frac{1}{3} \times 99 =$

4. What is the value of "n"? $(n \div 5) + 15 = 20$

   n = _____

5. Marcy has 2 cups that will hold 750 milliliters each. She also has a 2-liter bottle of water. If she completely fills each cup with water from the bottle, how much water will be left in the bottle?

   _____

Room Measurements	
Room	Measurements
1	10 meters x 8 meters
2	9 meters x 11 meters
3	7 meters x 12 meters
4	8 meters x 9 meters

Lesson 179

1. Look at the table. Which of the rooms has the greatest perimeter?

   _____

2. $3,100 \times 0.0002 =$

3. $\frac{5}{10} \times 200 =$

4. $(6 \times n) - 14 = 2 \times 2$
   n = _____

5. Kerry needs enough fencing to enclose a square garden that has 10-foot long sides. If the fencing is sold only in yards, how many yards of fencing will Kerry need to purchase? How do you know?

   _____

   _____

Room Measurements	
Room	**Measurements**
1	14 meters x 7 meters
2	10 meters x 10 meters
3	8 meters x 12 meters
4	11 meters x 9 meters

Lesson 180

1. Look at the chart. Which of the rooms has the smallest area?

   _____

2. $0.04 \times 21,000 =$

3. $\frac{3}{8} \times 40 =$

4. $(60 \div n) + 20 = 5 \times 6$
   n = _____

5. Daniel is putting a new floor in his kitchen. If his kitchen measures 10 feet by 10 feet, what is the area of the kitchen floor?

   _____

Room Measurements	
Room	**Measurements**
1	10 meters x 8 meters
2	9 meters x 11 meters
3	8 meters x 12 meters
4	11 meters x 9 meters

Answer Key: Lessons 1–16

Lesson 1
1. 214,589 + 2,000 = 216,589 buttons; answers will vary
2. 42
3. 3
4. 88
5. one thousands: 1; hundred thousands: 8; tens: 4; hundred millions: 5; ones: 3; ten thousands: 9; one millions: 7; hundreds: 2; ten millions: 6

Lesson 2
1. 400,000
2. 64
3. 3
4. 72
5. one thousands: 9; hundred thousands: 8; tens: 3; hundred millions: 4; ones: 5; ten thousands: 0; one millions: 6; hundreds: 1; ten millions: 2

Lesson 3
1. 8,218 cards
2. 16
3. 132
4. 5
5. one thousands: 3; hundred thousands: 0; tens: 4; hundred millions: 5; ones: 5; ten thousands: 9; one millions: 8; hundreds: 1; ten millions: 7

Lesson 4
1. 6 ten millions
2. 42
3. 72
4. 2
5. one thousands: 5; hundred thousands: 1; tens: 9; hundred millions: 8; ones: 3; ten thousands: 4; one millions: 0; hundreds: 6; ten millions: 2

Lesson 5
1. 6,594 wrappers
2. 7
3. 40
4. 70
5. one thousands: 1; hundred thousands: 8; tens: 4; hundred millions: 5; ones: 5; ten thousands: 2; one millions: 0; hundreds: 3; ten millions: 6

Lesson 6
1. C
2. 27
3. 56
4. 2
5. 534,926,817

Lesson 7
1. about 3,000 candies
2. 54
3. 3
4. 55
5. 901,836,306

Lesson 8
1. about 2,000 paper clips
2. 81
3. 1
4. 84
5. 914,563,278

Lesson 9
1. about 3,000 pages
2. 27
3. 56
4. 48
5. 620,891,443

Lesson 10
1. about 24,000 cookies
2. 45
3. 49
4. 96
5. 97,456,587

Lesson 11
1. 600,000,000 + 20,000,000 + 5,000,000 + 80,000 + 7,000 + 400 + 30 + 5
2. 30 books; answers will vary
3. 14
4. 4
5. 36

Lesson 12
1. 800,000,000 + 70,000,000 + 4,000,000 + 90,000 + 3,000 + 300 + 1
2. 50 candy bars; Add 4, subtract 1
3. 66
4. 4
5. 144

Lesson 13
1. 36
2. 64
3. 48
4. 704,016,038
5. 8; 12; 10; Add 4, subtract 2

Lesson 14
1. eight hundred ninety million two hundred fifty-eight thousand three
2. 81
3. 48
4. 45
5.

Lesson 15
1. 54
2. 49
3. 30
4. 400,000,000 + 9,000,000 + 200,000 + 90,000 + 4,000 + 6
5. 14; Add 2, rotate arrow right, add 2, rotate arrow up

Lesson 16
1. 400,000,000 + 90,000,000 + 600,000 + 20,000 + 8,000 + 70 + 1
2. 32
3. 40
4. 36
5. warmer day; answers will vary

Answer Key: Lessons 17–39

Lesson 17
1. 63
2. 32
3. 64
4. 460,910,301
5. 22; 25; add 3, add 3, star

Lesson 18
1. four hundred fifty-six million ninety-three thousand three hundred two
2. 63
3. 49
4. 12
5. 78° F; add 2° F per day

Lesson 19
1. 403,558,007
2. 90
3. 24
4. 108
5. 4,160; 8,320; Multiply by 2

Lesson 20
1. 70
2. 4
3. 9
4. 800,000,000 + 40,000,000 + 3,000,000 + 900,000 + 2,000 + 2
5. 420; 410; 1,230; Multiply by 3, subtract 10

Lesson 21
1. about $40 left
2. 45
3. 24
4. 28
5. 80; answers will vary

Lesson 22
1. $10.11
2. 4
3. 48
4. 6
5. a triangle

Lesson 23
1. $9.00
2. 5
3. 36
4. 5
5. 61 tickets

Lesson 24
1. 8
2. 132
3. 9
4. $200.00
5. $6.00

Lesson 25
1. $23.00
2. 54
3. 28
4. 81
5. yes; answers will vary

Lesson 26
1. a rectangle
2. 200
3. 1,200
4. 480
5. B

Lesson 27
1. answers will vary
2. 250
3. 2,400
4. 240
5. about 72,000 people

Lesson 28
1. circle; answers will vary
2. 350
3. 1,200
4. 120
5. 27

Lesson 29
1. 160
2. 250
3. 3,200
4. answers will vary
5. ⇨

Lesson 30
1. 30; even, and not a multiple of 11
2. about 1,500 people
3. 90
4. 180
5. 2,100

Lesson 31
1. a trapezoid
2. 5,600
3. 10,000
4. 1,800
5. 4 hours; answers will vary

Lesson 32
1. 5.5 hours
2. 3,500
3. 9,000
4. 1,600
5. a square

Lesson 33
1. 25 hours
2. 400
3. 36,000
4. 160
5. a diamond

Lesson 34
1. No, 5 min. late; answers will vary
2. 360
3. 10,000
4. 2,100
5. a rectangle

Lesson 35
1. 10 hours, 5 minutes
2. 1,400
3. 27,000
4. 2,400
5. a parallelogram

Lesson 36
1. yes
2. 60,000
3. 11
4. 10
5. (5, 2), (5, 0), and (1, 0)

Lesson 37
1. (2, 2) and (6, 3)
2. 120,000
3. 11
4. 12
5. $19.25

Lesson 38
1. $4.15
2. 200
3. 16,000
4. 30
5. (2, 4), (4, 4), and (3, 0)

Lesson 39
1. $15.00
2. 200,000
3. 11
4. 600
5. (6, 8) and (7, 4)

Answer Key: Lessons 40–60

Lesson 40
1. $5.00
2. (7, 4) and (8, 8)
3. 100,000
4. 11
5. 16,000

Lesson 41
1. Neither; they have eaten equal amounts.
2. 450
3. 122
4. 4,000
5. A and D; answers will vary

Lesson 42
1. 1,200
2. 7,500
3. 344
4. 3,000
5. B

Lesson 43
1. 411
2. 2,000,000
3. 200,000
4. Tina and Ramón
5.

Lesson 44
1. 1,060
2. 233
3. 70,000
4. 210,000
5. C, D, A, B, E

Lesson 45
1. 60,000,000
2. 342
3. 411
4. 4 pieces each
5. D

Lesson 46
1. B
2. 150
3. 45
4. 5
5. 140

Lesson 47
1. 6
2. 3
3. 240
4. 3,400
5. 20

Lesson 48
1. 7
2. 3.5
3. 30
4. 570
5. 6

Lesson 49
1. 1 pentagon, 5 triangles
2. 990
3. 84,000
4. 4,300
5. 150

Lesson 50
1. 5 rectangles, 2 pentagons
2. 1.5
3. 21
4. 170
5. 15

Lesson 51
1. Molly's Antiques; (5, 6)
2. $\frac{5}{10}$
3. 30,000
4. 8
5. 90

Lesson 52
1. A
2. 24 square centimeters
3. 150,000
4. 12
5. 156

Lesson 53
1. a cube; 6 square units
2. 2,000,000
3. 0.81
4. 4
5. $2.50

Lesson 54
1. 4.02
2. 300,000
3. 3
4. $\frac{3}{6}$
5. $8.00

Lesson 55
1. a square pyramid
2. 8.001
3. 12
4. 2,200,000
5. a square pyramid

Lesson 56
1. ⇨
2. 650,021,085
3. 40
4. 15
5. Erin; Stephie; Dena; Mia; Damara

Lesson 57
1. 60
2. 8.9
3. nine hundred eighty-eight million two hundred three thousand one
4. 2.01, 2.19, 9.12, 9.21
5.

Lesson 58
1. 800,000,000 + 400,000 + 30,000 +1,000 + 30
2. 111,000
3. 7,500
4. 5.09, 1.3, 0.95, 0.59
5.

Lesson 59
1. 448
2. 10,412,506
3. 9.79, 7.99, 7.09, 0.99
4. 50
5.

Lesson 60
1. 80,000,000 + 9,000,000 + 90,000 + 2,000 + 3
2. 50
3. 0.333; 1.03; 3.03; 3.3
4. 36
5.

Answer Key: Lessons 61–80

Lesson 61
1. 1,500,000
2. 15
3. 650
4. 10
5. 75° F; subtract 10° F, add 15° F

Lesson 62
1. $74.00; $9.00 increase per year
2. 350
3. 98
4. 60
5. 4 cubes

Lesson 63
1. 0
2. 30
3. 2.402
4. 1,200,000
5. 4,050.00; multiply by 10

Lesson 64
1. 80
2. 19.1
3. 4,200,000
4. $79.00; subtract $3.50
5. 120

Lesson 65
1. 90
2. 63.5
3. 330,000
4. $1,100; add 200, add 300
5. no; the box holds 800 cm³, but 1 m³ = 1,000,000 cm³

Lesson 66
1. $\frac{5}{8}$
2. 250
3. 28
4. 4^4
5. about 86; answers will vary

Lesson 67
1. $\frac{6}{7}$
2. $\frac{4}{9}$
3. 500
4. 44 feet
5. 30

Lesson 68
1. $\frac{11}{12}$
2. $\frac{3}{5}$
3. 120,000
4. 22
5. 20 inches

Lesson 69
1. 32 yards
2. $\frac{3}{20}$
3. 8.4
4. $\frac{11}{15}$
5. 33.5

Lesson 70
1. 8
2. 3,200
3. $\frac{5}{12}$
4. $\frac{2}{7}$
5. 14 cm

Lesson 71
1. 16 feet
2. 0.36
3. $\frac{5}{6}$
4. 33
5.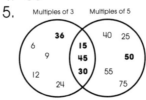

Lesson 72
1. 108
2. 0.64
3. $\frac{9}{10}$
4. 12, 24
5. 9 feet; radius is $\frac{1}{2}$ of diameter

Lesson 73
1. 17
2. 0.1002
3. 18 inches
4. 10, 20, 30, 40
5. $\frac{1}{2}$

Lesson 74
1. 89
2. 0.4008
3. no; answers will vary
4. $\frac{18}{25}$
5. 18, 36, 54

Lesson 75
1. 0.0666
2. 72
3. 6.25 inches
4. 21
5. $\frac{4}{19}$

Lesson 76
1. about $120; yes
2. 9
3. 0.12
4. $\frac{1}{3}$
5. Choco Delite; answers will vary

Lesson 77
1. 16
2. 0.00903
3. $\frac{5}{12}$
4. no
5. marigolds; answers will vary

Lesson 78
1. Cross Country; answers will vary
2. 0.007
3. $\frac{5}{12}$
4. 4
5. $30.00, $32.50, $35.00

Lesson 79
1. 0.0046
2. $\frac{3}{20}$
3. 5
4. no; answers will vary
5. 38, 35, 70; multiply by 2, subtract 3

Lesson 80
1. 0.0101
2. $\frac{5}{19}$
3. 1
4. 93, 94; multiply by 3, add 1
5. 4 yards; answers will vary

Answer Key: Lessons 81-100

Lesson 81
1. in a rectangle, end-to-end
2. 0.7
3. 13
4. $\frac{1}{3}$
5. Moe, Chris, José, Harold, Bryson

Lesson 82
1. in a square
2. 0.0095
3. 31
4. $\frac{3}{20}$
5. 2nd, 4th, 1st, 3rd

Lesson 83
1. $\frac{11}{15}$
2. 0.089
3. 9
4. in a long rectangle
5. Rick, Mick, Dan, Jon

Lesson 84
1. 12
2. 9
3. 1.06
4. $\frac{1}{3}$
5. 5; 1; 4; 2; 3

Lesson 85
1. $\frac{3}{10}$
2. 1.83
3. 17
4. 10
5. 9.2, 9.04, 8.5, 8.09, 3.1, 1.03

Lesson 86
1. 1
2. $\frac{1}{7}$
3. 50
4. yellow; answers will vary
5. D

Lesson 87
1. yellow; answers will vary
2. $\frac{1}{4}$
3. 80
4. 10
5. B

Lesson 88
1. orange; answers will vary
2. $\frac{2}{5}$
3. 150
4. 1
5. A

Lesson 89
1. a ten; answers will vary
2. 160
3. $\frac{13}{20}$
4. 9
5. F

Lesson 90
1. a fork; answers will vary
2. $\frac{1}{2}$
3. 300
4. 4
5. E

Lesson 91
1. nickels
2. 0.104
3. 15,000
4. $5\frac{1}{2}$
5. 330

Lesson 92
1. $5\frac{2}{3}$
2. 0.122
3. 2,400
4. 10 dimes, 1 quarter, 1 penny
5. 700

Lesson 93
1. yes
2. 0.075
3. 7,500
4. $20\frac{4}{5}$
5. 100

Lesson 94
1. yes; answers will vary
2. $5\frac{1}{3}$
3. 0.39
4. 18,000
5. no

Lesson 95
1. 0.54
2. $31\frac{3}{4}$
3. 8,000
4. $1.62
5. 56

Lesson 96
1. 2.1
2. $3\frac{4}{7}$
3. $\frac{1}{2}$
4. Bill
5. multiply by 4

Lesson 97
1. Mark
2. 2.73
3. $2\frac{1}{8}$
4. $\frac{1}{4}$
5. subtract 2

Lesson 98
1. $\frac{1}{3}$
2. $13\frac{3}{4}$
3. 0.4
4. Lucas; answers will vary
5. 5N

Lesson 99
1. Arcella; answers will vary
2. 0.8
3. $3\frac{5}{9}$
4. $4\frac{10}{11}$
5. 3N

Lesson 100
1. 95, 94; subtract 1, multiply by 5.
2. N − 5
3. 60
4. $1\frac{3}{4}$
5. $2\frac{3}{10}$

Answer Key: Lessons 101–120

Lesson 101
1. 2,000,000
2. 5
3. 100
4. 70°
5.

Lesson 102
1. 2,200,000
2. 20
3. 33
4. 360°
5. ☐ ; [cube]

Lesson 103
1. 200,000
2. 8
3. 48
4. 360°
5. ⟹

Lesson 104
1. 300,000
2. 5
3. 7.5
4. 30°
5. 5 ; ☐

Lesson 105
1. 40,000
2. 7
3. 3,600
4. 90°
5. ⟹

Lesson 106
1. 12
2. $6\frac{1}{4}$
3. $4\frac{1}{2}$
4. the red bucket
5. Number of Keys: 11, 13; Number of Key Rings: 5, 6

Lesson 107
1. 25
2. $7\frac{1}{2}$
3. $5\frac{2}{5}$
4. yes; answers will vary
5. Cups of Nuts: $2\frac{1}{2}$, 3; Number of Recipes: 5, 6

Lesson 108
1. yes; answers will vary
2. 12
3. $9\frac{2}{5}$
4. $7\frac{1}{12}$
5. 11; 13; 33; 39

Lesson 109
1. 4
2. $13\frac{2}{3}$
3. 250
4. $12\frac{1}{2}$
5. N + 6

Lesson 110
1. 36
2. $10\frac{2}{3}$
3. 7
4. 6.5
5. 20; 24; 40; 48

Lesson 111
1. 2
2. 0.105
3. $\frac{4}{5}$
4. 3
5. 12; 16; 20; 5 bags of chocolate chips

Lesson 112
1. 2
2. 0.275
3. 1
4. 1
5. 20; 25; 24; 29

Lesson 113
1. 20
2. $\frac{2}{3}$
3. 0.0203
4. 3,000
5. 125; 625; 250; 1,250

Lesson 114
1. 6
2. 0.0606
3. 1
4. 1,050
5. 44; 42; 22; 21

Lesson 115
1. 2
2. 1.002
3. $\frac{2}{3}$
4. 1,200
5. 30; 20; 3; 2

Lesson 116
1. 7
2. 8
3. 2
4. 4
5. 8

Lesson 117
1. 21
2. 4
3. 10
4. 14
5. 11

Lesson 118
1. 3
2. 10
3. 6
4. $\frac{5}{8}$
5. $\frac{1}{8}$

Lesson 119
1. 7
2. 25
3. 32
4. 500
5. yes; she will arrive in 56 minutes

Lesson 120
1. 10
2. 3
3. 8
4. 25
5. 5 cars

Answer Key: Lessons 121–143

Lesson 121
1. 932,402,387
2. 8
3. 2
4. 20 feet; answers will vary
5. 6 cm; 4 cm

Lesson 122
1. 518,390
2. $1\frac{3}{7}$
3. 18
4. 7
5. 32

Lesson 123
1. 294,838,951
2. 4
3. $2\frac{2}{5}$
4. 36 meters
5. 30 in.

Lesson 124
1. 390,293,342
2. 8
3. $2\frac{3}{11}$
4. 8 meters
5. 15 inches

Lesson 125
1. 873,483,903
2. 45
3. $1\frac{3}{4}$
4. 50 inches
5. 7 cm

Lesson 126
1. 4
2. 17
3. 50
4. 10
5. 16

Lesson 127
1. 9
2. 9
3. 4
4. 100
5. 90

Lesson 128
1. 7; 5; 13
2. 4
3. 4
4. 300
5. 280

Lesson 129
1. 99
2. 10
3. 40
4. 6
5. 480

Lesson 130
1. 10 ÷ 2 = 5
2. 15
3. 2
4. 120
5. 914

Lesson 131
1. 0.8
2. 1; 2; 3; 6
3. forty-three million ninety-eight thousand seven hundred six
4. Monique
5. 3

Lesson 132
1. 0.25
2. 1; 2; 5; 10
3. 303,004,201
4. 22; 19; 38
5. $\frac{5}{9}$

Lesson 133
1. 0.4
2. 1; 5; 25
3. twenty-nine million three hundred one thousand two
4. 310; 312; 1,560
5. $\frac{7}{8}$

Lesson 134
1. 10
2. 1; 2; 4; 8; 16; 32; 64
3. 405,222,003
4. 27; 54; 55
5. $\frac{3}{5}$

Lesson 135
1. 0.25
2. 1; 2; 3; 4; 6; 8; 12; 24
3. thirty-two million, ninety thousand, four hundred twelve
4. $\frac{3}{8}$
5. 4 and 5

Lesson 136
1. 12
2. 10
3. 90,000
4. T; answers will vary
5. 81

Lesson 137
1. 30
2. 64
3. 24,000
4. the spinner with two 1s and two 3s; answers will vary
5. 100

Lesson 138
1. 63
2. 33
3. 80
4. $\frac{3}{5}$
5. $\frac{2}{5}$

Lesson 139
1. 24
2. 50
3. 7.5
4. $\frac{5}{9}$
5. $\frac{4}{9}$

Lesson 140
1. 60
2. 150
3. 0.016
4. $\frac{3}{4}$
5. $\frac{1}{4}$

Lesson 141
1. 12
2. 12
3. 1; 2; 4; 8; 16; 32
4. 3,500
5. 60

Lesson 142
1. 4
2. 45
3. 1; 2; 4; 7; 8; 14; 28; 56
4. 100
5. 24

Lesson 143
1. 13
2. 36, 72, 108
3. 1; 3; 17; 51
4. 550
5. 88

Answer Key: Lessons 144–163

Lesson 144
1. 324
2. 10, 20, 30
3. 1; 2; 7; 14; 28
4. 1,500
5. 98

Lesson 145
1. 24
2. 12
3. 1; 5; 9; 45
4. 16
5. 12

Lesson 146
1. 40
2. Jill; answers will vary
3. $\frac{7}{4}$
4. $3\frac{1}{2}$
5. Donica, Miranda, Chris, Lario, Erika, Damon

Lesson 147
1. $1\frac{4}{5}$
2. $5\frac{1}{5}$
3. 42
4. Monica; answers will vary
5. 8.01; 3.91; 3.12; 3.09; 0.99

Lesson 148
1. $\frac{9}{4}$
2. $2\frac{1}{2}$
3. 60
4. 45
5. 3.4; 4.03; 8.1; 9.14; 9.2

Lesson 149
1. $\frac{8}{5}$
2. 10
3. 1; 2; 4; 11; 22; 44
4. 6
5. 2.03, 2.1, 3.04, 3.2, 4.8, 4.90

Lesson 150
1. $1\frac{2}{5}$
2. $5\frac{1}{2}$
3. 1; 23
4. neither ran farther
5. 10.4, 10.09, 5.90, 5.3, 4.25, 4.01

Lesson 151
1. 51 circled
2. 3
3. 80,000
4. 85; answers will vary
5. Answers will vary

Lesson 152
1. 17
2. 15
3. 17 circled
4. 24
5. 3,000,000

Lesson 153
1. 45 circled
2. 10
3. 3,600
4. 30
5. 25

Lesson 154
1. 23 circled
2. 6
3. 2,400
4. 28
5. 26

Lesson 155
1. 19 circled
2. 10
3. 8,000
4. 100
5. 32.1

Lesson 156
1. $\frac{3}{5}$
2. $\frac{1}{4}$
3. 2,000,000,000
4. $\frac{1}{4}$
5. 8; answers will vary

Lesson 157
1. $\frac{5}{9}$
2. $8\frac{5}{14}$
3. 3,000,000,000
4. $\frac{5}{9}$
5. 48; answers will vary

Lesson 158
1. $2\frac{5}{8}$
2. 9
3. 7,500
4. $8.50; $9.00
5. $\frac{1}{7}$

Lesson 159
1. $2\frac{11}{12}$
2. 9
3. 9,100,000
4. $\frac{2}{5}$
5. 38.5; 66

Lesson 160
1. 19
2. $12\frac{1}{2}$
3. $7\frac{1}{3}$
4. $\frac{1}{2}$
5. 76; 67

Lesson 161
1. no; answers will vary
2. 90
3. $\frac{3}{4}$
4. $\frac{1}{3}$
5. cube or rectangular prism; pentagonal pyramid

Lesson 162
1. yes; answers will vary
2. $\frac{2}{3}$
3. $4\frac{3}{5}$
4. 750
5. 8

Lesson 163
1. no; answers will vary
2. 11
3. $7\frac{1}{2}$
4. 0.27
5. 18

Answer Key: Lessons 164–180

Lesson 164
1. no
2. $8\frac{1}{2}$
3. 16
4. 2
5. a cube; answers will vary

Lesson 165
1. no; answers will vary
2. 15
3. 14
4. 400,000
5. both have 8

Lesson 166
1. 1,350
2. yes
3. $\frac{1}{9}$, $\frac{1}{7}$, $\frac{1}{5}$, $\frac{1}{4}$, $\frac{1}{3}$
4. 0.15
5. 8

Lesson 167
1. 1,500
2. 0.5
3. $\frac{3}{12}$, $\frac{3}{10}$, $\frac{3}{9}$, $\frac{3}{5}$, $\frac{3}{4}$
4. yes; answers will vary
5. 100s; answers will vary

Lesson 168
1. 7,200,000
2. 0.408
3. 5.4, 4.5, $3\frac{1}{2}$, 1.2, 1.02
4. $\frac{3}{4}$ hours
5. 90; 85; 80; 75; 70; 65; 60; 55

Lesson 169
1. 6,300
2. 0.0066
3. $4\frac{1}{2}$, 4.6, $5\frac{1}{2}$, 9.05, 9.5
4. $1\frac{1}{2}$
5. 1 hour and 45 minutes

Lesson 170
1. 60,000
2. 0.0027
3. $\frac{1}{4}$, $\frac{1}{2}$, $\frac{6}{8}$, $\frac{8}{8}$
4. 2,500
5. Answers will vary

Lesson 171
1. 50
2. 5.555
3. $\frac{1}{7}$
4. $\frac{6}{13}$
5. Week 2

Lesson 172
1. 42
2. 0.065
3. $\frac{1}{5}$
4. $\frac{1}{2}$
5. $\frac{2}{3}$

Lesson 173
1. $\frac{2}{9}$
2. 330
3. $18\frac{1}{5}$
4. $\frac{1}{5}$
5. $\frac{2}{5}$

Lesson 174
1. $7\frac{1}{12}$
2. 9.1
3. 10
4. B
5. A

Lesson 175
1. $54\frac{3}{5}$
2. 1,220
3. 2
4. 5th graders
5. Pizza

Lesson 176
1. 3,600
2. 5
3. Living Room
4. 30,000
5. 60

Lesson 177
1. Office 2
2. 0.0091
3. 20
4. 150
5. 6,500

Lesson 178
1. Room 4
2. 108
3. 33
4. 25
5. 500 milliliters

Lesson 179
1. Room 1
2. 0.62
3. 100
4. 3
5. 14 yards; answers will vary

Lesson 180
1. Room 1
2. 840
3. 15
4. 6
5. 100 square feet

Assessment 1 (Lessons 1–10)

Name _____

What place value is held by the 2 in the following numbers?

1. 875,201,345

A. hundreds
B. thousands
C. ten thousands
D. hundred thousands

2. 109,420,578

A. hundreds
B. thousands
C. ten thousands
D. hundred thousands

3. 923,684,531

A. thousands
B. ten thousands
C. ten millions
D. hundred millions

4. 6 x 9 =

A. 45
B. 72
C. 56
D. 54

5. 7 x 9 =

A. 63
B. 72
C. 45
D. 54

6. 8 x 7 =

A. 54   B. 56
C. 72   D. 63

Use the following graph to answer questions 7 and 8.

Charlie and 4 of his friends collect bumper stickers when they travel. They formed a club called the "Bumper Sticker Bonanza." The number of bumper stickers each member of the club has collected is shown in the chart below.

Bumper Stickers Collected

Team Member	Number of Stickers
Charlie	2,890
Shar	1,798
Benny	3,125
Monica	2,790
Juana	4,023

7. About how many bumper stickers have Charlie and Juana collected altogether?

A. 6,000
B. 8,000
C. 7,000
D. 9,000

8. Who has collected about 2,000 bumper stickers?

A. Monica
B. Charlie
C. Shar
D. Juana

Assessment 2 (Lessons 11–20)

Name _____

1. 5,000,000 + 20,000 + 3,000 + 600 + 1 =

  A. 5,023,610
  B. 5,203,601
  C. 5,020,361
  D. 5,023,601

2. 6 x 7 =

  A. 56
  B. 42
  C. 63
  D. 72

3. 8 x 6 =

  A. 56
  B. 42
  C. 48
  D. 72

4. Which is the expanded form of 460,801?

  A. 400,000 + 60,000 + 800 + 1
  B. 400,000 + 6,000 + 800 + 1
  C. 400,000 + 60,000 + 80 + 1
  D. 40,000 + 6,000 + 800 + 1

5. Which number shows 8 millions, 4 thousands, 3 tens, and 2 ones?

  A. 800,400,032
  B. 8,004,032
  C. 8,040,302
  D. 80,004,320

6. Which number shows 90 millions, 6 hundred thousands, 8 thousands, and 4 ones?

  A. 90,608,040
  B. 900,600,804
  C. 90,608,004
  D. 9,608,004

Use the following graph to answer questions 7 and 8.

Benny runs every day to build his endurance for the cross country team. The graph shows the distances he ran on 5 different days.

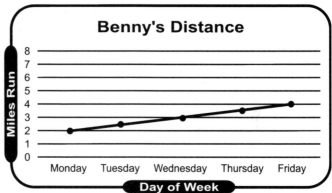

7. Benny ran 7.5 miles on which 2 days combined?

  A. Monday and Wednesday
  B. Tuesday and Thursday
  C. Thursday and Friday
  D. Monday and Friday

8. Based on the data, how many miles would you predict Benny would run on Saturday?

  A. 5 miles
  B. 4.5 miles
  C. 4 miles
  D. 6 miles

Assessment 3 (Lessons 21–30)

Name _____

1. 9 x 7 =

A. 72
B. 63
C. 81
D. 56

2. 6 x 8 =

A. 72
B. 54
C. 48
D. 56

3. 9 x 8 =

A. 72
B. 54
C. 81
D. 56

4. Estimate the answer.
   189,103 + 504,200 =

A. 600,000
B. 500,000
C. 800,000
D. 700,000

5. Which is the expanded form of
   87,054,100?

A. 80,000,000 + 7,000,000 + 50,000 +
   4,000 + 10
B. 800,000,000 + 70,000,000 + 50,000
   + 4,000 + 100
C. 800,000,000 + 7,000,000 + 50,000 +
   4,000 + 100
D. 80,000,000 + 7,000,000 + 50,000 +
   4,000 + 100

Use the following information to
answer questions 6 through 8.

Timmerman's Sale Prices	
Item	**Cost**
T-shirts	3 for $10.00 (sold in 3s)
Shorts	$5.00 per pair
Slides	$7.00 per pair
Basketballs	$12.00 each
Tennis Shoes	$30.00 per pair

6. Rob has $50.00. What could he
   purchase and have change?

A. 1 pair of tennis shoes, 1 set of
   T-shirts, and 2 pairs of shorts
B. 2 pairs of slides, 2 sets of T-shirts,
   and 3 pairs of shorts
C. 4 sets of T-shirts and 2 pairs
   of shorts
D. 1 pair of tennis shoes and 4 pairs
   of shorts

7. About how much would 3 pairs
   of shorts and 2 basketballs cost?

A. $50
B. $45
C. $40
D. $25

8. If Rob spent $24 and bought 3
   items, what did he purchase?

A. 1 pair of shorts, 1 set of T-shirts,
   and 1 pair of slides
B. 1 pair of shorts, 1 pair of slides,
   and 1 basketball
C. 1 basketball, 1 set of T-shirts, and 1
   pair of slides
D. 2 pairs of slides and 1 basketball

Assessment 4 (Lessons 31–40)

Name _____

1. 8 x 9 =

A. 63
B. 72
C. 56
D. 81

2. 6 x 9 =

A. 56
B. 72
C. 54
D. 48

3. 20 x 30 =

A. 600
B. 60
C. 6,000
D. 500

4. 600 x 10 =

A. 600
B. 60
C. 6,000
D. 60,000

5. 77 ÷ 7 =

A. 10
B. 17
C. 1
D. 11

Use the following information to answer questions 6 through 8. Andre is going to take a walk in his new neighborhood in Shapeville. He has a map to help him find his way. Use the following grid to answer questions about Andre's adventure.

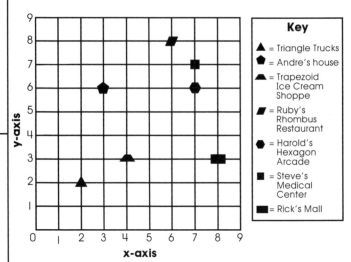

6. Andre begins his journey at home. At what coordinates is his home?

A. (6,3)
B. (3,6)
C. (2,6)
D. (6,2)

7. Andre's first stop is at (2,2). What business is located there?

A. Trapezoid Ice Cream Shoppe
B. Harold's Hexagon Arcade
C. Triangle Trucks
D. Ruby's Rhombus Restaurant

8. Andre stops for lunch at Ruby's Rhombus Restaurant. He wants to continue his adventure and decides his next stop will be Rick's Mall. The most direct route from Ruby's to Rick's would be:

A. (6,8) to (6,9) to (10, 9) to (10,3) to (8,3)
B. (6,8) to (5,7) to (5,3) to (8,3)
C. (6,8) to (5,8) to (5,5) to (8,5) to (8,3)
D. (6,8) to (6,3) to (8,3)

Assessment 5 (Lessons 41–50)

Name _____

1. 9,800 x 0.01 =

A. 98
B. 980
C. 98,000
D. 980,000

2. 605 ÷ 5 =

A. 101
B. 131
C. 121
D. 131

3. 7,700 ÷ 70 =

A. 110
B. 1,100
C. 10
D. 11,000

4. What shape will this net, or pattern, make?

A. rectangle
B. tetrahedron
C. pyramid
D. cube

5. Order the following numbers from least to greatest.
   2,348,201   2,342,804
   2,438,408   2,248,408

A. 2,348,201, 2,342,804, 2,438,408, 2,248,408
B. 2,248,408, 2,438,408, 2,342,804, 2,348,201
C. 2,248,408, 2,342,804, 2,438,408, 2,348,201
D. 2,248,408, 2,342,804, 2,348,201, 2,438,408

Use the coordinate grid to answer questions 6 through 8.

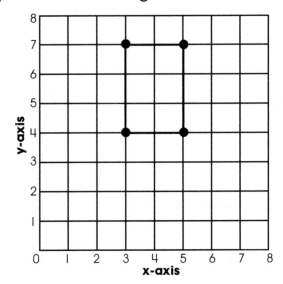

6. What are the coordinates of the rectangle in the grid?

A. (4,3), (4,7), (7,5), (7,7)
B. (3,4), (3,6), (5,4), (5,7)
C. (3,4), (3,7), (5,4), (5,7)
D. (3,4), (3,7), (4,4), (5,7)

7. If the rectangle were rotated $\frac{1}{4}$ turn to the right, what would the new coordinates be?

A. (5,4), (5,7), (8,4), (8,7)
B. (4,4), (4,7), (8,4), (8,7)
C. (5,4), (5,6), (8,4), (8,6)
D. (5,4), (5,6), (7,4), (7,7)

8. Slide the rectangle down so that the coordinates of the bottom, left corner are (3,3). What are the rectangle's new coordinates?

A. (3,3), (6,3), (6,5), (6,6)
B. (3,3), (3,6), (5,3), (5,6)
C. (3,3), (5,3), (6,5), (5,5)
D. (3,3), (6,3), (5,5), (5,6)

Assessment 6 (Lessons 51–60)

Name _____

1. 20,000 x 0.02 =

   A. 4,000
   B. 400
   C. 40
   D. 400,000

2. 80,000 ÷ 0.01 =

   A. 8,0000
   B. 8000
   C. 800
   D. 8,000,000

3. 10,000 x 0.025 =

   A. 2,500
   B. 250
   C. 25
   D. 2.5

4. 250,000 ÷ 0.025 =

   A. 100,000
   B. 10,000,000
   C. 10,000
   D. 100

5. $\frac{3}{7} = \frac{n}{14}$
   n = _____

   A. 6
   B. 7
   C. 9
   D. 14

Use the frequency chart to answer questions 6 through 8.

Mrs. Thomas gave a multiplication test. The scores and finish times for 5 of her students are listed below.

Mrs. Thomas' Class Scores

Student	Score	Time (in minutes)
Bryson	80	2.05
Eugene	95	3.15
Nina	95	2.1
Becca	100	2.95
Doug	90	3.1

6. Which student finished first?

   A. Nina
   B. Becca
   C. Bryson
   D. Doug

7. In which order did the students finish the test?

   A. Bryson, Nina, Becca, Doug, Eugene
   B. Bryson, Becca, Nina, Doug, Eugene
   C. Eugene, Doug, Becca, Nina, Bryson
   D. Eugene, Becca, Doug, Nina, Bryson

8. What is the range of the finish times?

   A. 1.05 minutes
   B. 8.50 minutes
   C. 1.10 minutes
   D. 1.01 minutes

Assessment 7 (Lessons 61–70)

1. $6 \times (3 + 1) =$

   A. 18
   B. 19
   C. 24
   D. 20

2. $(4 \times 5) \times 0.01 =$

   A. 20
   B. 0.20
   C. 2
   D. 0.02

3. $2,000 \times 0.30 =$

   A. 600
   B. 60
   C. 6
   D. 0.6

4. $\frac{1}{4} + \frac{1}{4} =$

   A. $\frac{2}{8}$

   B. $\frac{2}{16}$

   C. $\frac{1}{16}$

   D. $\frac{1}{2}$

5. $\frac{5}{8} + \frac{1}{8} =$

   A. $\frac{3}{4}$

   B. $\frac{6}{16}$

   C. $\frac{5}{16}$

   D. $\frac{6}{64}$

6. What is the average of the following numbers?
   45, 69, 22, 71, 38

   A. 49
   B. 42
   C. 38
   D. 50

7. What is the perimeter of the square?

   28 yards

   A. 102 yards
   B. 120 yards
   C. 112 yards
   D. 140 yards

8. Look at the stem and leaf chart. What is the highest math score?

   A. 89
   B. 95
   C. 100
   D. 99

Math Scores	
9	2 5 9
8	3 4 8 9
7	0 5 8
6	6 7

Assessment 8 (Lessons 71–80)

Name _____

1. $2.3 \times 0.2 =$

A. 46
B. 4.6
C. 0.46
D. 0.046

2. $\frac{4}{4} = \frac{n}{20}$
   n = _____

A. 16
B. 20
C. 4
D. 12

3. $\frac{2}{7} + \frac{3}{7} =$

A. $\frac{5}{15}$

B. $\frac{2}{7}$

C. $\frac{1}{14}$

D. $\frac{5}{7}$

4. $\frac{8}{9} - \frac{3}{9} =$

A. $\frac{5}{0}$

B. $\frac{1}{18}$

C. $\frac{5}{9}$

D. $\frac{5}{18}$

5. Which number is a common multiple of 4 and 6?

A. 2
B. 18
C. 12
D. 16

Use the following table to answer questions 6 through 8.

Andy's mom went to the store to purchase several items. This is her list. The cost of each item includes tax.

Grocery List	
Bread	$1.90
Cereal	$3.10
Milk	$2.80
Soda	$6.00
Meat	$5.20

6. About how much money would Andy's mom need to make her purchases?

A. $25.00   B. $15.00
C. $20.00   D. $30.00

7. Put the items in order from the least cost to the greatest cost.

A. Milk, bread, cereal, soda, meat
B. Bread, milk, cereal, meat, soda
C. Bread, milk, cereal, soda, meat
D. Milk, bread, meat, soda, cereal

8. If Andy's mom has $18.00, will she have enough money? If she does have enough money, how much change will she receive?

A. Yes; $1.00 change
B. Yes; $1.50 change
C. Yes; $0.50 change
D. No; she needs $1.00

Assessment 9 (Lessons 81–90)

Name _____

1. $\frac{7}{12} - \frac{2}{12} =$

A. $\frac{3}{12}$

B. $\frac{4}{12}$

C. $\frac{3}{0}$

D. $\frac{5}{12}$

2. $8.5 \times 0.02 =$

A. 17
B. 1.7
C. 0.17
D. 0.017

3. $4.6 \div 0.2 =$

A. 23
B. 2.3
C. 0.23
D. 0.023

4. $18.9 \div 0.03 =$

A. 0.630
B. 6.30
C. 630
D. 6,300

5. $0.8 = \frac{n}{5}$
   n = _____

A. 1
B. 2
C. 3
D. 4

Use the spinner to answer questions 6 through 8.

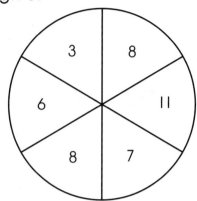

6. If Emma spins the spinner 1 time, what are her chances of spinning an 8?

A. $\frac{2}{3}$ B. $\frac{1}{6}$

C. $\frac{1}{4}$ D. $\frac{1}{3}$

7. If Emma spins the spinner 1 time, what are her chances of not spinning an even number?

A. $\frac{5}{6}$ B. $\frac{1}{2}$

C. $\frac{3}{4}$ D. $\frac{1}{4}$

8. If Emma spins the spinner 1 time, what are her chances of spinning an odd number between 1 and 9?

A. $\frac{1}{5}$ B. $\frac{2}{5}$

C. $\frac{3}{4}$ D. $\frac{1}{3}$

Assessment 10 (Lessons 91–100)

Name _____

1. $5\frac{1}{3} + 2\frac{1}{3} =$

   A. $5\frac{2}{3}$

   B. $7\frac{2}{6}$

   C. $7\frac{2}{3}$

   D. $3\frac{2}{3}$

2. $6.1 \times 0.02 =$

   A. 122
   B. 0.122
   C. 1.22
   D. 12.2

3. Cassie wants to purchase a book for $5.25. She has 2 dollar bills, 7 quarters, 14 dimes, and 6 nickels. Does Cassie have enough money to purchase the book? If so, how much change will she have left?

   A. Yes, with $0.25 in change
   B. No, with no change
   C. Yes, with $0.20 in change
   D. Yes, with $0.15 in change

4. $\frac{6}{15} - \frac{4}{15} =$

   A. $\frac{2}{0}$

   B. $\frac{2}{15}$

   C. $\frac{10}{15}$

   D. $\frac{10}{0}$

5. $8\frac{3}{10} - 4\frac{2}{10} =$

   A. $4\frac{5}{10}$

   B. $4\frac{3}{10}$

   C. $4\frac{2}{10}$

   D. $4\frac{1}{10}$

6. $15,000 \times 0.001 =$

   A. 15
   B. 150
   C. 1,500
   D. 1.5

7. Martin and Marcy run laps around the track every day. If Martin can runs 4 laps in 12 minutes and Marcy can run 5 laps in 10 minutes, who will reach a total of 40 laps first, and why?

   A. Marcy, because it will take her 120 minutes to run 40 laps.
   B. Martin, because it will take him 80 minutes to run 40 laps.
   C. Martin, because it will take him 120 minutes to run 40 laps.
   D. Marcy, because it will take her 80 minutes to run 40 laps.

8. Dean made the following scores in math class last semester: 80, 40, 75, 75, 100, 85, 85, and 100. What is his average score?

   A. 85
   B. 80
   C. 75
   D. 70

1. $6\frac{1}{3} + \frac{3}{3} =$

    A. $6\frac{2}{3}$

    B. $6\frac{1}{3}$

    C. $5\frac{1}{3}$

    D. $7\frac{1}{3}$

2. $\frac{1}{5} \times 35 =$

    A. 5
    B. 7
    C. 6
    D. 8

3. $0.50 \times 200 =$

    A. 100
    B. 10
    C. 0.10
    D. 0.01

4. $930,000,000 \div 300 =$

    A. 31,000
    B. 310,000
    C. 3,100,000
    D. 31,000,000

5. $9\frac{5}{25} - 4\frac{2}{25} =$

    A. 5

    B. $4\frac{3}{25}$

    C. $5\frac{3}{25}$

    D. $5\frac{0}{25}$

6. What is "n"? $n \times 20 = 10$

    A. 10
    B. 0.5
    C. 2.5
    D. 15

7. Jenny makes bracelets for her friends. The following chart shows how many beads she needs for different kinds of bracelets. Based on the data in the chart, how many beads does Jenny need for an 8-inch bracelet?

Jenny's Bracelets						
Bracelet Size (in inches)	$3\frac{1}{2}$	4	$4\frac{1}{2}$	5	$5\frac{1}{2}$	6
Number of Beads	10	14	19	25	32	40

    A. 75
    B. 82
    C. 85
    D. 92

8. Look at the pattern below. What is the rule?
    3, 6, 5, 10, 9, 18, 17, 34 . . . .

    A. Add 4 to the first number and subtract 1 from the next number.
    B. Multiply the first number by 3 and add 1 to the next number.
    C. Add 4 to the first number and multiply the next number by 2.
    D. Multiply the first number by 2 and subtract 1 from the next number.

Name _____

1. What is the value of "n"? $n^2 = 25$

   A. 20
   B. 5
   C. 10
   D. 2

6. $5.5 \times 0.02 =$

   A. 0.11
   B. 1.1
   C. 11
   D. 110

2. $\frac{2}{7} + 1\frac{3}{7} =$

   A. $1\frac{5}{7}$

   B. $\frac{5}{7}$

   C. $1\frac{5}{14}$

   D. $\frac{5}{14}$

3. What is the value of "n"?
   $2 + (n - 5) = 21 \div 3$

   A. 4
   B. 7
   C. 8
   D. 10

4. $\frac{4}{5} \times 30 =$

   A. 120
   B. 150
   C. 6
   D. 24

5. $\frac{8}{9} - \frac{3}{9} =$

   A. $\frac{5}{18}$

   B. $\frac{5}{0}$

   C. $\frac{5}{9}$

   D. $\frac{11}{18}$

Use the information below to answer questions 7 and 8. The graph represents the percentage of different entrees eaten by fifth graders last week. A total of 520 fifth graders ate lunch each day.

**Entrées
Eaten**

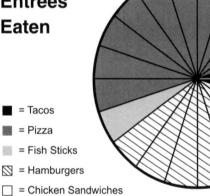

■ = Tacos
▨ = Pizza
▢ = Fish Sticks
▨ = Hamburgers
▢ = Chicken Sandwiches

7. How many fifth graders ate pizza last week?

   A. 130
   B. 260
   C. 65
   D. 400

8. How many fifth graders ate tacos and chicken sandwiches last week?

   A. 130
   B. 104
   C. 90
   D. 25

Name _____

1. The sum of which number sentence is a prime number?

   A. $7 + 7 =$
   B. $8 + 7 =$
   C. $9 + 8 =$
   D. $9 + 9 =$

2. The sum of which number sentence is a composite number?

   A. $9 + 4 =$
   B. $9 + 9 =$
   C. $8 + 9 =$
   D. $11 + 12 =$

3. $\frac{3}{5} \times 40 =$

   A. 24
   B. 8
   C. 32
   D. 16

4. Look at the following numbers. Which number has the smallest digit in the ten thousands place?

   372,892   928,531,895
   849,093   4,304,291

   A. 4,304,291
   B. 849,093
   C. 928,531,895
   D. 372,892

5. What is the value of "n"?
   $12 - (2 \times n) = n \times 2$

   A. 1
   B. 2
   C. 3
   D. 0

6. $\frac{7}{12} + \frac{4}{12} =$

   A. $\frac{11}{24}$

   B. $\frac{10}{12}$

   C. $\frac{5}{6}$

   D. $\frac{11}{12}$

Use the coordinate grid to answer questions 7 and 8.

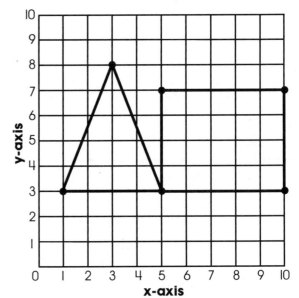

7. Which coordinates form a line of symmetry for the triangle?

   A. (3,3) and (3,8)
   B. (1,3) and (3,8)
   C. (1,4) and (3,8)
   D. (3,1) and (3,9)

8. Which coordinates are shared by the triangle and the rectangle?

   A. (3,5)
   B. (5,3)
   C. (1,3)
   D. (3,1)

Assessment 14 (Lessons 131–140)

Name _____

1. $\frac{2}{5}$ = _____

A. 0.2
B. 0.4
C. 0.6
D. 0.8

2. 0.25 = _____

A. $\frac{1}{2}$ B. $\frac{1}{3}$

C. $\frac{1}{4}$ D. $\frac{1}{5}$

3. 0.15 x 10,000,000 =

A. 1,500,000
B. 150,000
C. 15,000
D. 1,500

4. What is the standard form of the number?
50,000,000 + 400,000 + 30,000 + 2,000 + 60 + 9

A. 50,432,069
B. 50,430,269
C. 54,030,269
D. 54,032,069

Use the following information to solve questions 5 through 8.

Patti has a bag with 20 pieces of candy in it. All of the pieces of candy are the same size. There are 5 milk chocolates, 6 peppermints, 7 dark chocolates, and 2 spearmints.

5. If Patti reaches into the bag, what are her chances of randomly pulling out a spearmint candy first?

A. $\frac{2}{10}$ B. $\frac{2}{20}$

C. $\frac{5}{20}$ D. $\frac{1}{2}$

6. If Patti reaches into the bag, what are her chances of randomly pulling out a piece of chocolate candy first?

A. $\frac{5}{20}$ B. $\frac{7}{20}$

C. $\frac{3}{10}$ D. $\frac{3}{5}$

7. If Patti reaches into the bag, what are her chances of randomly pulling out a piece of mint candy first?

A. $\frac{3}{5}$ B. $\frac{7}{20}$

C. $\frac{2}{5}$ D. $\frac{7}{10}$

8. If Patti reaches into the bag, what are her chances of randomly pulling out something other than a spearmint candy?

A. $\frac{3}{10}$ B. $\frac{11}{20}$

C. $\frac{9}{20}$ D. $\frac{9}{10}$

Name _____

1. $8\frac{2}{5} - 6\frac{1}{5} =$

A. $1\frac{4}{5}$

B. $2\frac{1}{5}$

C. $2\frac{1}{10}$

D. $1\frac{1}{10}$

2. Which number is greater, $\frac{8}{6}$ or $1\frac{1}{2}$?

A. Neither; they are equal.

B. $\frac{8}{6}$

C. $1\frac{1}{2}$

D. They cannot be compared.

3. What are the factors of 18?

A. 1, 2, 3, 6, 9, 18
B. 1, 2, 3, 4, 6, 9
C. 1, 3, 4, 6, 9
D. 1, 2, 3, 6, 9

4. What is the least common multiple of 3 and 7?

A. 14
B. 21
C. 28
D. 42

5. $8\frac{4}{8} - 6\frac{1}{8} =$

A. $2\frac{3}{8}$

B. $1\frac{3}{8}$

C. $2\frac{3}{16}$

D. $1\frac{3}{16}$

6. $9 + (5^2 - 1) \div 11 =$

A. 2
B. 9
C. 11
D. 3

Use the graph below to solve questions 7 and 8.

The graph shows the number of minutes it takes each member of the Norton family to brush his or her teeth.

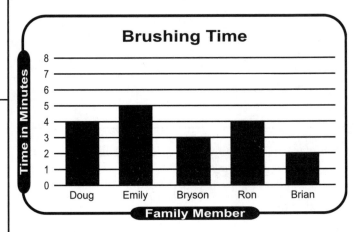

Brushing Time

7. What is the mode of this graph?

A. 4 minutes
B. $4\frac{1}{2}$ minutes
C. $3\frac{1}{2}$ minutes
D. $5\frac{1}{2}$ minutes

8. What is the range of this graph?

A. 3 minutes
B. 4 minutes
C. $4\frac{1}{2}$ minutes
D. 5 minutes

Assessment 16 (Lessons 151–160)

Name _____

1. $4\frac{2}{10} + 24\frac{3}{10} =$

A. $20\frac{1}{10}$

B. $28\frac{1}{2}$

C. $28\frac{1}{20}$

D. $20\frac{5}{10}$

2. $\frac{3}{8} \times 24 =$

A. 6
B. 9
C. 4
D. 3

3. $35,000,000 \times 0.005 =$

A. 1,750,000
B. 175,000
C. 17,500
D. 1,750

4. $4\frac{7}{8} - 2\frac{4}{8} =$

A. $2\frac{6}{8}$

B. $6\frac{9}{8}$

C. $2\frac{3}{8}$

D. $2\frac{3}{0}$

5. $84,000 \div 0.002 =$

A. 42,000,000
B. 4,200,000
C. 420,000
D. 42,000

6. The quotient of which number sentence is a composite number?

A. $51 \div 3 =$
B. $26 \div 2 =$
C. $10 \div 2 =$
D. $24 \div 2 =$

7. The difference of which number sentence is a prime number?

A. $72 - 10 =$
B. $35 - 18 =$
C. $45 - 15 =$
D. $100 - 50 =$

8. Every fifth house on Amanda's block is painted green. There are 10 houses on Amanda's block. What are the chances that Amanda does not live in a green house?

A. $\frac{8}{10}$

B. $\frac{5}{8}$

C. $\frac{7}{10}$

D. $\frac{1}{5}$

1. $\frac{9}{11} + \frac{1}{11} =$

   A. $\frac{10}{22}$

   B. $\frac{8}{22}$

   C. $\frac{10}{11}$

   D. $\frac{8}{11}$

2. $4\frac{2}{5} - 1\frac{1}{5} =$

   A. $2\frac{1}{5}$

   B. $3\frac{1}{5}$

   C. $2\frac{0}{5}$

   D. $3\frac{0}{5}$

3. $80{,}000 \times .05 =$

   A. 4,000,000   B. 400,000
   C. 40,000   D. 4,000

4. $4.5 \times 0.2 =$

   A. 0.9   B. 9
   C. 90   D. 900

5. Order the following fractions from least to greatest.

   $\frac{2}{8} \quad \frac{2}{4} \quad \frac{2}{6} \quad \frac{2}{3} \quad \frac{2}{5}$

   A. $\frac{2}{3} \quad \frac{2}{4} \quad \frac{2}{5} \quad \frac{2}{6} \quad \frac{2}{8}$

   B. $\frac{2}{3} \quad \frac{2}{5} \quad \frac{2}{6} \quad \frac{2}{4} \quad \frac{2}{8}$

   C. $\frac{2}{8} \quad \frac{2}{6} \quad \frac{2}{5} \quad \frac{2}{4} \quad \frac{2}{3}$

   D. $\frac{2}{8} \quad \frac{2}{6} \quad \frac{2}{5} \quad \frac{2}{3} \quad \frac{2}{4}$

Use the data to answer questions 6 through 8.

Mattie's uncle catches fish for a living. The following graph shows the number of pounds of fish Uncle Pablo caught every day last week.

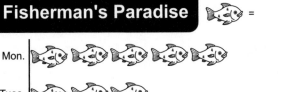

Fisherman's Paradise

6. If Uncle Pablo caught 900 pounds of fish on Tuesday, how many pounds of fish does each fish picture represent?

   A. 300   B. 400
   C. 500   D. 600

7. How many pounds of fish did Uncle Pablo catch last week?

   A. 5,000   B. 7,500
   C. 1,000   D. 1,250

8. Uncle Pablo will fish again on Saturday. Based on the pattern of the data, about how many fish should he expect to catch?

   A. about 500   B. about 750
   C. about 1,000 D. about 1,500

Assessment 18 (Lessons 171–180)   Name _____

1. $\frac{5}{8} \times 40 =$

A. 20
B. 25
C. 30
D. 35

2. 6.6 x 1.01 =

A. 6.666
B. 6.66
C. 6.6
D. 6

3. $7\frac{8}{9} - 4\frac{4}{9} =$

A. $3\frac{12}{18}$

B. $3\frac{5}{9}$

C. $3\frac{4}{9}$

D. $11\frac{9}{12}$

4. 6,500 x 0.02 =

A. 150
B. 140
C. 130
D. 120

5. What is the value of "n"?
    $(60 \times 2) - n = n + 60$

A. 30
B. 40
C. 50
D. 60

Use the information below to answer questions 6 through 8.

Laurie is helping her little brother identify shapes. She has put all of the shapes below in a box. Her brother must close his eyes, pick out a shape to identify, then return it to the box.

6. If Laurie's brother chooses one shape from the box, what are his chances of choosing a circle?

A. $\frac{3}{14}$ B. $\frac{5}{14}$

C. $\frac{4}{11}$ D. $\frac{2}{7}$

7. If Laurie's brother chooses one shape from the box, what are his chances of choosing something with more than 3 straight edges?

A. $\frac{3}{14}$ B. $\frac{1}{2}$

C. $\frac{11}{14}$ D. $\frac{5}{14}$

8. If Laurie's brother chooses one shape from the box, what are his chances of choosing something that has no curves?

A. $\frac{5}{7}$ B. $\frac{2}{7}$

C. $\frac{7}{14}$ D. $\frac{11}{14}$

Assessment Answer Keys

Assessment 1
1. D
2. C
3. C
4. D
5. A
6. B
7. C
8. C

Assessment 2
1. D
2. B
3. C
4. A
5. B
6. C
7. C
8. B

Assessment 3
1. B
2. C
3. A
4. D
5. D
6. B
7. C
8. B

Assessment 4
1. B
2. C
3. A
4. C
5. D
6. B
7. C
8. D

Assessment 5
1. A
2. C
3. A
4. D
5. D
6. C
7. C
8. B

Assessment 6
1. B
2. D
3. B
4. B
5. A
6. C
7. A
8. C

Assessment 7
1. C
2. B
3. A
4. D
5. A
6. A
7. C
8. D

Assessment 8
1. C
2. B
3. D
4. C
5. C
6. C
7. B
8. D

Assessment 9
1. D
2. C
3. A
4. C
5. D
6. D
7. B
8. D

Assessment 10
1. C
2. B
3. C
4. B
5. D
6. A
7. D
8. B

Assessment 11
1. D
2. B
3. A
4. C
5. C
6. B
7. B
8. D

Assessment 12
1. B
2. A
3. D
4. D
5. C
6. A
7. B
8. B

Assessment 13
1. C
2. B
3. A
4. A
5. C
6. D
7. A
8. B

Assessment 14
1. B
2. C
3. A
4. A
5. B
6. D
7. C
8. D

Assessment 15
1. B
2. C
3. A
4. B
5. A
6. D
7. A
8. A

Assessment 16
1. B
2. B
3. B
4. C
5. A
6. D
7. B
8. A

Assessment 17
1. C
2. B
3. D
4. A
5. C
6. A
7. B
8. D

Assessment 18
1. B
2. A
3. C
4. C
5. A
6. D
7. B
8. A

Real World Application 1

One mile equals 5,280 feet. How many laps around your classroom will it take to equal a mile? How do you know?

_____ laps

_____

_____

_____

_____

_____

_____

Real World Application 2

Mauro found $0.75 in his pocket. In the space below, list all of the possible combinations of coins that Mauro may have found.

Real World Application 3

Survey your classmates to find everyone's favorite color. Create a line plot graph and a circle graph to show the data you have collected. Next, compare the two graphs. Which graph displays the information more effectively? Explain your answer.

Real World Application 4

Think of two buildings in your community. In the space below, create nets to show what shapes make up each building.

Real World Application 5

Your teacher has asked you to estimate the total number of books in your classroom (or your school library). How will you get the correct answer? In the space below, explain your strategy for making an accurate estimate.

_____

_____

_____

_____

_____

_____

Real World Application 6

Could you create a circle with a radius of 11 feet in your classroom? Why or why not?

_____

_____

_____

_____

_____

Real World Application 7

Fill in the calendar to match the current month. Write important dates on your calendar. How many patterns can you find?

Sunday	Monday	Tuesday	Wednesday	Thursday	Friday	Saturday

Real World Application 8

Record the high and low temperatures for ten school days. Find the average high and low temperatures for that ten-day period.

High and Low Temperatures Over Ten-Day Period

Day	High Temp.	Low Temp.	Day	High Temp.	Low Temp.

Average High: _____   **Average Low:** _____

Name _____

Real World Application 9

Choose 8 pieces of furniture in your classroom. Create a coordinate grid showing their locations.

Real World Application 10

If you had $20.00 to spend on anything, what would you purchase? Go to a store with a family member or friend. Make a list of items whose total cost (before taxes) is exactly $20.00.

Items/# Purchased	Price Per Item	Total Item Cost
1. _____	_____	_____
2. _____	_____	_____
3. _____	_____	_____
4. _____	_____	_____
5. _____	_____	_____
6. _____	_____	_____
7. _____	_____	_____
8. _____	_____	_____
9. _____	_____	_____

Total Cost _____ _____

Daily Math Warm-Ups Grade 5

Real World Application 11

Draw four polygons on a separate piece of paper to create a set. Think of a reason why each shape might not belong to the set. Justify your answers.

_____

_____

_____

_____

_____

_____

_____

Real World Application 12

Make up an original word problem involving a variable with the value of "n" and write it on the lines below. Write the answer in the box. Have a classmate try to solve your word problem.

_____

_____

_____

_____

_____